MATCH ANNUAL 2

D1145031

TAKEN FROM THE PAGES OF MATCH facts

MATCH ANNUAL 2002 MANAGING EDITOR Chris Hunt ART DIRECTOR Darryl Tooth EDITOR Ian Foster ASSISTANT EDITOR Bev Ward WRITERS Kevin Hughes, Giles Milton, Katherine Hannah PRODUCTION EDITOR James Bandy SUB-EDITORS Richard Adams, Kevin Pettman SENIOR DESIGNER Becky Booth DESIGNERS Martin Barry, Calum Booth, Leyton Edwards STAFF PHOTOGRAPHER Phil Bagnall CONTRIBUTORS Daniel Ferguson-Thomas, Russ Carvell AND THE REST OF THE MATCH TEAM Hugh Sleight, Dawn Brown, Lloyd Rogers, Richard Ecclestone

MATCH BRITAIN'S BIGGEST & BEST FOOTBALL MAGAZINE

Bushfield House, Orton Centre, Peterborough PE2 5UW ★ Tel: 01733 237111
Fax: 01733 288150 ★ e-mail: match.magazine@emap.com

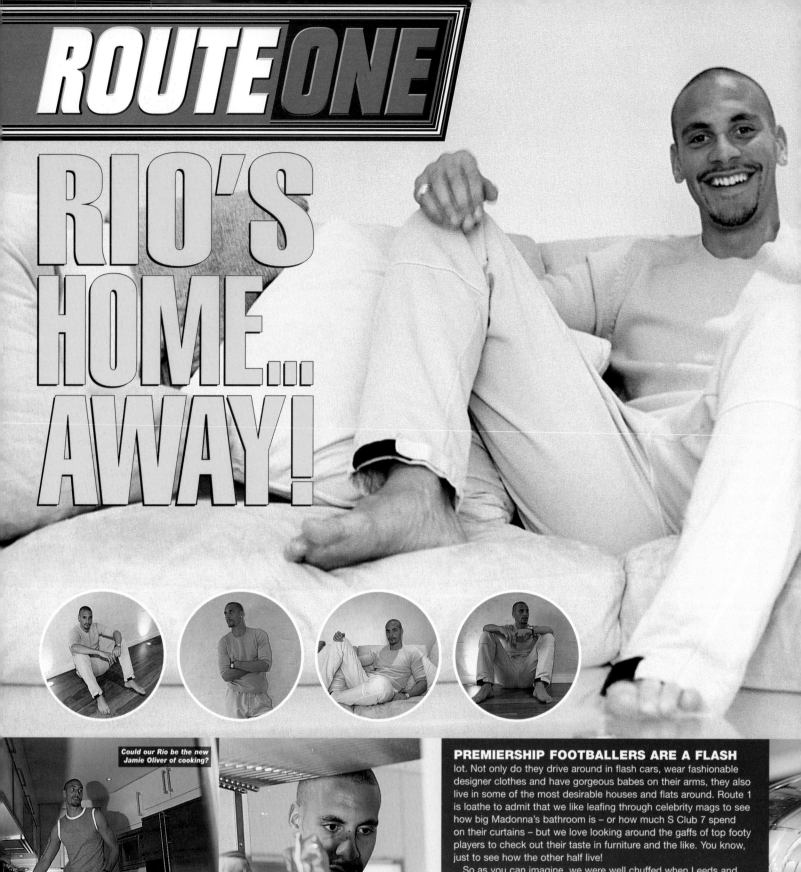

ROUTE ONE

RIO'S HOME... AWAY!

Could our Rio be the new Jamie Oliver of cooking?

"This is my pukka stir fry – cool new catchphrase, eh?"

PREMIERSHIP FOOTBALLERS ARE A FLASH lot. Not only do they drive around in flash cars, wear fashionable designer clothes and have gorgeous babes on their arms, they also live in some of the most desirable houses and flats around. Route 1 is loathe to admit that we like leafing through celebrity mags to see how big Madonna's bathroom is – or how much S Club 7 spend on their curtains – but we love looking around the gaffs of top footy players to check out their taste in furniture and the like. You know, just to see how the other half live!

So as you can imagine, we were well chuffed when Leeds and England defender Rio Ferdinand invited Route 1 for an exclusive snoop around his pad when he was back in London for a couple of days. The former West Ham star, who hails from Peckham, still keeps his apartment in the capital as well as his place in Yorkshire, which means he still gets to see family and friends. **"I was brought up in Peckham so I still hang out with all my old mates"** Rio told Route 1. **"You can't just ditch your mates because you're in the limelight and the newspapers. My family wouldn't let it happen and I haven't been brought up to do anything like that. If you become a big-head on the field, it'll go wrong for you off it."**

So what did we think? Very flash – that's what was in our minds as we walked over the wooden floors, complete with up-lighting, and into the chrome interior kitchen. Certainly not learning his skills from Laurence Llewelyn-Bowen, of 'Changing Rooms' fame, Rio's apartment is the ultimate in footballer's cool. We did ask him if he would come up to MATCH Towers to advise us on some new office furniture, but he mumbled something about the UEFA Cup…

PAOLO DI BOSSIO!

When the time comes for the eccentric Paolo di Canio to pack away his footy boots, what's he gonna do with the rest of his life? The West Ham striker, as usual, couldn't wait to express his plans. **"Maybe, if there is a crazy chairman who will give me a manager's job, then I'll be a manager,"** he gesticulated to Route 1. **"It's something I've considered and it interests me, but I'm not ready yet. All I want to do is play football, that's all I want to think about. I still have 100 per cent of my energy left and I want to give something very special to the West Ham supporters."** Your flash car would be something very special to give them mate!

PR Tips

Words of wisdom from Sunderland's tea-drinking gaffer

Champions League? How about a ******* Chimpions League, la?

COLES' LAW

England's Cole men are on a mission to rewrite the footy law books. But what can the stars do this time?

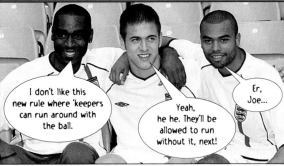

I don't like this new rule where 'keepers can run around with the ball.

Yeah, he he. They'll be allowed to run without it, next!

Er, Joe...

CHELSEA'S EXCLUSION BLUES

Chelsea got their fancy Kings Road knickers all in a twist when they heard that the powerful G14 group of top European clubs was set to be expanded – leaving Chelsea behind. The footy consortium, which includes Manchester United and Liverpool, have a big influence in the European game and the boys down at The Bridge don't want to be left in the cold. **"G14, if it is going to be the real voice of the big clubs, must be expanded,"** boomed The Blues' MD Colin Hutchinson. **"On European results over recent years, Arsenal, Leeds and ourselves should be in."** Yeah, Chelsea's defeat to Swiss no-hopers St. Gallen in last season's UEFA Cup should just about swing it for you, Hutch!

IT'S TRAINING MEN!

Newcastle have already got wildly passionate supporters, a massive stadium and a squad full of expensively-acquired stars so what could they possibly be missing? Route 1 was a little bit surprised to here the answer from their captain Alan Shearer. **"The next thing we need here is a training ground because we haven't got our own yet and we need to have that,"** Al told Route 1. **"With everything else that's going on, a training ground is very important. The stadium is second to none and it's what the Newcastle people deserve, but we've got to give them something to shout about now."** How many fans are going to shout about a fancy training ground? Give them a trophy Al!

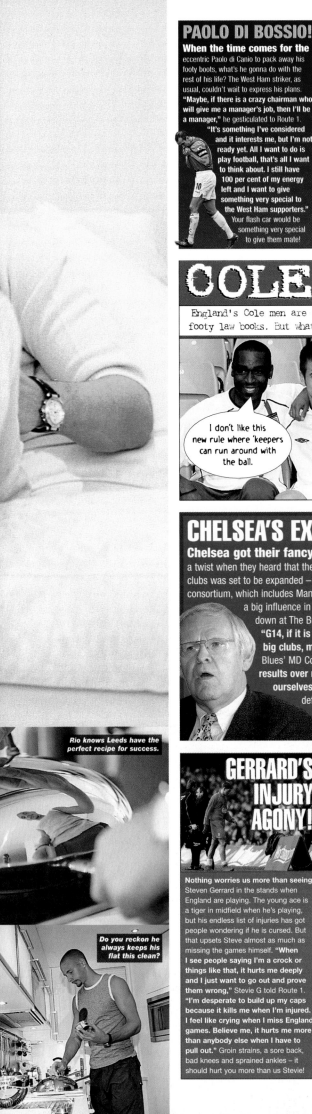

Rio knows Leeds have the perfect recipe for success.

Do you reckon he always keeps his flat this clean?

GERRARD'S INJURY AGONY!

Nothing worries us more than seeing Steven Gerrard in the stands when England are playing. The young ace is a tiger in midfield when he's playing, but his endless list of injuries has got people wondering if he is cursed. But that upsets Steve almost as much as missing the games himself. **"When I see people saying I'm a crock or things like that, it hurts me deeply and I just want to go out and prove them wrong,"** Stevie G told Route 1. **"I'm desperate to build up my caps because it kills me when I'm injured. I feel like crying when I miss England games. Believe me, it hurts me more than anybody else when I have to pull out."** Groin strains, a sore back, bad knees and sprained ankles – it should hurt you more than us Stevie!

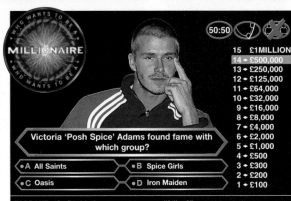

15	£1MILLION
14	£500,000
13	£250,000
12	£125,000
11	£64,000
10	£32,000
9	£16,000
8	£8,000
7	£4,000
6	£2,000
5	£1,000
4	£500
3	£300
2	£200
1	£100

Victoria 'Posh Spice' Adams found fame with which group?

A All Saints — B Spice Girls
C Oasis — D Iron Maiden

TARRANT: "So David, do you want to use a lifeline?"
BECKHAM: "Can I phone a friend? Can I call Victoria?"
TARRANT: "Sure. (Phone rings) Hello Victoria, this is Chris Tarrant on 'Who Wants To Be A Millionaire?'. The next voice you hear will be David Beckham's."
BECKHAM: "Hi Princess."
VICTORIA: "Hello David, what's the problem?"
BECKHAM: "I'm on 'Who Wants To Be A Millionaire?' I don't know whether to use a lifeline or not?"
VICTORIA: "Two fings, David. You're already using a lifeline. Second, baby, is that we're multi-millionaires already. We don't need any more cash."
BECKHAM: "Oh yeah. Love you…"

SKOOL DAYZ

Shay Given
Newcastle United

Route 1 cheekily asks the stars to turn back the clock and reveal what they used to get up to at school!

FAVOURITE SUBJECT
"Metalwork – a man's subject! I don't really know if I would have made a career out of it but it was something I enjoyed."

FAVOURITE TEACHER
"I didn't really have a favourite teacher. I guess it would be my PE teacher, who also managed the school football team. He was a good laugh with us."

LEAST FAVOURITE SUBJECT
"Singing in music wasn't my favourite at all. I don't think it was the most popular thing among any of the lads!"

LEAST FAVOURITE TEACHER
"Oh, I don't want to say anyone for this, you never know – they might come looking for me!"

HOMEWORK
"I was known to copy a bit of homework on the bus on the way to school in my time. But who hasn't done that?"

SCHOOL UNIFORM
"It wasn't that bad actually. It was black trousers and a grey jumper. We didn't have to wear shorts, so it wasn't too bad!"

PHYSICAL EDUCATION
"I don't know if I was one of the best at PE. There were a couple of lads in my class and we were maybe a bit better than the rest."

DETENTION
"I never had detention once in four years of senior school. I'm very proud of that record, I don't know how I escaped it but yeah, I'm very proud of that! I just got away with things a bit more than most by ducking and diving!"

SCHOOL DINNERS
"We had packed lunch. I used to make my own ham sandwiches!"

POKEYMEN

#131 Duncandonut
TYPE: Monster

Description
Duncandonut is possibly the toughest Pokeyman of all time. Anyone with common sense will approach him with caution. He's prone to smashing up those who venture into his natural habitat and can turn any part of his body into a weapon, particularly his head. Although he sounds too good to be true, he is rarely found in action due to a severe condition where parts of his body regularly fall off. If you can keep him together, he will be a wonderful capture.

First seen: Episode 8, 'Can't play, won't play'

Route 1's ongoing series. The FA's gotta charge 'em all!

NOT TO BE CONFUSED...

Oh, I do feel like people walk all over me sometimes, you know.

Sol Campbell   **Old campbed**

YOUTH COLE!

In recent years, Arsenal have been slated for having a rubbish youth system, or at least not paying any attention to the players that come through it. But that's rubbish according to their exciting young English defender Ashley Cole! **"We've got a good youth set-up at Arsenal – there are quite a few youngsters in the reserves, like Graham Barrett, who should do well,"** he told Route 1. **"I think there should be a couple of English players in the team, but the foreigners have done so well that you can't knock them."** True, but you can always make fun of their silly dress sense and funny names!

FANTASY FOOTBALL FIGHTS

It's the greatest footy players ever – Pelé v Maradona!

The all-time bout – who is the toughest old duffer? Along with MATCHMAN tonight is Dutch legend Johan Cruyff.

MATCHMAN: "It's the big one, the one we've all been waiting for. The All-Time Champion Heavyweight belt! Pelé 'The Pulveriser' v Diego 'Fists of God' Maradona. Both claim to be the greatest, but who'll walk away with the trophy? What do you think Johan?"
CRUYFF: "For sure they are both talented. They were perhaps not as good as me, no?"
MATCHMAN: "Wow! Controversial words there! And the bell's gone. Maradona's tottering towards Pelé. He doesn't look in very good shape though."
CRUYFF: "Too many beef steaks have made Diego a big boy, huh?"
MATCHMAN: "Maybe, but Pelé is looking old. This could be over quickly! Maradona's weaved through Pelé's defence and caught him. An amazing attack!"
CRUYFF: "I'm thinking it is not bad. For sure, I could do better."
MATCHMAN: "Both are showing some of their old moves."
CRUYFF: "It looks like Maradona is taking some pills…"
MATCHMAN: "Just look at his eyes. That's some spinach! He's lifted Pelé in the air. This has got to be all over, but wait… "
CRUYFF: "For all the tulips in Amsterdam! What is that?"
MATCHMAN: "A giant hand is coming down from above! It's crushed Maradona! Dirty Diego's been crushed by the Hand Of God!"
CRUYFF: "For sure, but I was just as good in my time…"
MATCHMAN: "An amazing end. Pelé is champion, Maradona is a fleshy pulp. The crowd loves it! Thank you ladies and gentlemen, and goodnight!"

It's all kicking off!

UNITED'S

The groundsman is kept busy with 14 pitches to look after!

When you are the biggest, you tend to demand the best. So the fact that Manchester United have one of the flashiest training grounds around won't come as a big surprise. Fancy a look at it? Well, welcome to Route 1's guided tour of the Carrington training ground!

United's old training ground, The Cliff, was starting to become a bit decrepit, to say the least. So £14 million was spent on the new facility, which was completed in January 2000. Situated in Carrington, six miles from Old Trafford, it covers 70 acres of land, with 14 training pitches of various sizes and surfaces. But it isn't just about that. Inside the main building is a large swimming pool, physio and massage rooms and a variety of saunas. You'll also find weights rooms, a restaurant and even squash and basketball courts to keep the players fit and entertained.

Carrington has also been designed with extra-curricular facilities in mind. It boasts conference rooms, classrooms and offices, a media room and a MUTV studio, where interviews with the players are recorded every day. In fact, it's got pretty much anything you could ever wish for – except maybe a good chip shop! **"It has some fantastic facilities,"** United defender Gary Neville told Route 1 as he pounded one of the treadmills in the flash fitness centre. **"As you can see, it's right up there with any training ground in the world."** Who are we to argue? There are many fantastic new training grounds popping up all over Britain, but it seems United are once again leading the way in terms of quality.

Roy Keane gets his muscles from working out here!

Becks and co have lunch in the canteen.

GREGORY'S BOYS ARE HAPPY!

Aston Villa boss John Gregory looks like the most terrifying man in football. Not only is he ruthless, strict, abrupt and gobby, he also dresses like one of Al Capone's henchmen and rides a motorbike! But as Gareth Barry told Route 1, he's a joy to work with, even though he still has a go now and again! **"I've enjoyed working with him – he's given me the chance to be involved at a young age,"** Gazza Bazza explained. **"He gets straight to the point. If he thinks something's not right he'll let you know. But equally, if things are going well, he'll let you get on with it and give you encouragement."** Unless you're David Ginola. In which case, he'll kick you in the teeth!

NEW GROUND!

Carrington: A top training facility for the top footy team in England.

The players can relax after training in the flash lounge.

The swimming pool helps treat injuries.

Giggsy spends a fair amount of time in here.

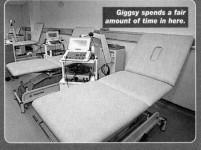

Wes Brown tries to get out of doing the weights!

TINY REDKNAPP?

Jamie Redknapp's England Under-15 footy career wasn't one of the greatest of all time. The Liverpool midfielder played just one game for the young England side but despite all his skills, he just wasn't big enough! **"I went to all the trials as a schoolboy, but at that age I was a late developer and very small, one of the smallest there,"** he admitted to Route 1. **"There were other kids that weren't technically better than me but stronger on the pitch. When I went to the trials I got down to the last 20 but didn't quite make it. But then I got a call from Dave Burnside, who was managing the side. He said, 'Would you come down to the game?'. I played, got a cap and you can't take that away."** We wouldn't dare Jamie!

STICK AT IT, SAYS BARRY!

Glasgow Rangers hardly get a round of applause when they visit opposition grounds and the man who takes most of the stick is usually young captain Barry Ferguson. But although he's the player fans love to hate, Ferguson says he doesn't mind it at all because it spurs him on to do even better! But why do opposition fans dislike him? **"It's because I'm Scottish,"** he decided, remembering that he's one of the few homegrown players to actually grace the Rangers first team. **"I can handle all the stick. You just have to live with it. I don't mind it because it's part of football. I enjoy getting a bit of stick really, it helps you raise your game!"** Hmm, we're sure opposing supporters will now keep quiet for you Baz – not!

CROSS TRAINING!

Middlesbrough – the best in the entire world? Not the football team, obviously, but Boro say their training ground facilities are the best around, even better than United's (see opposite)! And, as goalkeeper Mark Crossley told Route 1, wherever they are in the league, they're always up for a bit of training. **"The club reckons the training facilities here are among the best in the world, and when you arrive in the morning it does makes you feel like training,"** Crossley told us. **"The pitches are like Wembley so you just couldn't hope for a better place to come. There's enough room to put 11 national teams on there. I believe they're making the big house at the front into a huge hotel. Anyone who comes to visit will be impressed by the facilities."** Yeah, it's just a shame you can't say that about the players!

my favourite... BOOK

DON HUTCHISON
SUNDERLAND

SO DON, WHAT ARE YOU READING?
"I read the Paolo di Canio autobiography recently – that was a really good read."

WHAT WAS YOUR FAVOURITE PART?
"I liked the bits about his early days when he was a young Lazio fan in Rome. He had some good stories."

SO WHAT ABOUT 'DON: THE AUTOBIOGRAPHY'?
"I'll probably do one some time in the future. I haven't really got enough to write about yet, but I'll let you know when I do!"

THE LITERARY WORLD AWAITS!

RANIERI LEFT IN THE DARK AGAIN!

Okay-a so who forgot to pay-a the electricity bill?

KING FOR A DAY

Matt Jansen
Blackburn Rovers

King Matt reveals to **Route 1** what he'd do if he ruled the nation!

Who would you have knighted?
"My dad's really helped me out in my career, but I wouldn't knight him coz he'd get a big head! I don't know, maybe Steve Coppell who used to be my manager when I was at Crystal Palace. He really helped me out a lot before I went to Blackburn Rovers."

Who would you have beheaded?
"I think my mate Giles for his rollerblading in Central Park! I went over to New York last year with him and we were in Central Park rollerblading and he was ridiculous, falling over all the time – arms and legs everywhere, he was really quite unbelievable. It was like Bambi on ice, so I'd behead him for embarrassing us!"

Who would be your queen?
"Meg Ryan. I quite like some of the films that she's done but I also think she's really good looking – that's the main reason I watch anything she's in. I think she would make a great queen alongside me!"

Who would be your servant?
"Either my agent, Jay, because he's always running around after me – making sure I'm doing what I'm supposed to do and being where I'm meant to be. Or my mum could be my servant, she's always looked after me really well!"

What would you eat?
"Maybe fillet steak, or I really like a Chinese takeaway, so I could go for that, too. To be honest, I'm a hopeless cook. I can only do beans on toast or a pot noodle, but my sister lives next door to me and she makes sure I don't starve or anything! There are lots of good Chinese takeaway places around here though, so I've been to those quite a few times."

high 5ive

LEE HUGHES
west brom

TOP FIVE...
SPORTS OTHER THAN FOOTY

1. Snooker
2. Golf
3. Formula 1
4. Boxing
5. Basketball

WE'RE THE BEST!

No longer shall we listen to whinging football 'experts' who moan about how bad the English are at football. True footy expert Gerard Houllier says we have an abundance of top youngsters at our disposal. **"English football has a reservoir of young talent,"** said Houllier. **"There's Cole and Carrick at West Ham and the players we have at Liverpool. By the 2006 World Cup, you should have an England team capable of great things. Most of the big countries have 20 top-quality young players, but England have perhaps 40 coming through!"** Not so Gerard – if you'd read MATCH's Top Teenagers feature you'd know there are at least 50 starlets ready to cause a stir in English footy!

Rile Niall

Football's biggest bovver-boys queue up to try to wind-up Sunderland's genial Irishman.

This Week
ROY KEANE

ROY KEANE: "Who told yer you could be a professional footballer, eh? Yer look more like a basketball player to me, yer lanky idjut."

NIALL SAYS: "Aye to be sure, you're right dat I haven't got the greatest physique. But as Shaquille O'Neill told me the other day when I beat him in a one-on-one, a basketball career just wouldn't be a challenge for me, so it wouldn't."

VIEIRA AND HENRY

NIKE SHOX

Henry hopes to take his form on the football pitch onto the basketball court.

"Thierry, watch, you do this..."

"Patrick, the basket iz so high, you must help me!"

"...and it goes up and into ze hoop."

COOL CAPTAIN BARRY!

'If you can keep your head while all others around you are losing theirs, you'll be a man' – so says the famous poem by Rudyard Kipling. And it seems that while many Aston Villa players have been struggling to perform at their best, young defender Gareth Barry has improved his game and shown the level head that Kipling bumbled on about. So is he as calm as he appears on the pitch? **"I'm nervous before every match,"** admitted Barry. **"I think it helps a little bit if the first things you do in a game are simple and easy – that gets the nerves out of your body."** Even so, the assured left-footer just keeps getting better and already has an eye on the role that would make him the main man at Villa Park. **"I'm still young and I would like to improve every aspect of my defending. It'd be nice if I stayed at Villa long enough to become captain."** There's a quicker way than that, Gazza – just give your skipper a boot in training!

SLAM JAM!

Vieira wonders whether his mate will ever understand the rules!

These boys are only used to dunking their biscuits!

"It iz easy to get ze three points in zis game, non?"

It was the one-on-one that they'd all been waiting for. Forget Alton Byrd v Michael Jordan, Kobe Bryant v Allen Iverson, or any other all-star basketball match you could ever dream off. This was the matchup of matchups – Arsenal stars Patrick Vieira and Thierry Henry in a three-point shootout, with Route 1 refereeing the whole encounter!

Arsenal's star shooter threw first – and if you thought Henry was deadly in the Premiership, believe us – it's nothing compared to his accuracy at the hoop. Vieira followed and wasn't to be outdone by his compatriot, dropping the ball in with a cry of delight. Game on!

Thierry's next two throws went straight in, as did Vieira's... but then drama! Henry's fourth effort hit the rim of the basket, rolled right around and came out. So Patrick had the upper hand. He calmly looped his next shot into the hoop, followed by a nervy Henry effort.

If Vieira made his next shot, he would win. So with all the physique and grace of a pro basketball player, he bent his knees, flicked his wrists and threw. Almost in slow motion, the ball looped, hit the back of the basket, rolled around, balanced on the edge... and dropped in! Thierry fell to his knees in despair. Vieira had won 5-4. Slamdunk da funk!

ROBBIE'S SOMERSAULT SECRET

Every football fan in the land must be able to describe how Robbie Keane celebrates his goals by now. Sprinting away, the Leeds marksman flips into a somersault (a bit of a dodgy one, to be fair), then finishes off by cocking his finger in a nifty salute. Cheeky. But, Route 1 demands to know, what's the meaning of the whole thing? **"It's just one of the things I used to do when I was a kid,"** revealed Keano with a whisper. **"I used to do the same somersault then, and they say you should never alter your winning ways so I'm certainly not going to change now. It's something I've always done, for as long as I can remember. I can't say for sure how old I was when I started doing it."** Oh, not *that* impressive, then – if you've had a decade or so to practise, shouldn't you be 'saulting through hoops of fire and balancing your nose by now as well? Get to work on it Robbie mate!

TEDDY'S NO CANTONA!

Teddy Sheringham's contributions to Man. United's title-winning campaign last season were pretty flash. But since he moved to Tottenham people have been making comparisons with United's number one hero, legend Eric Cantona. But there shouldn't even be a comparison according to Gary Neville. **"I wouldn't compare Teddy Sheringham to Eric Cantona,"** he told Route 1. **"Teddy's far more of a team player than Eric was – you can never compare anyone to Eric. Teddy is a bigger team player and Eric was an individual who produced the ridiculous, if you like, but he had amazing talent and I would never compare anyone to him."** Not even God? Surely he's close...

WHAT'S IN A (NICK)NAME?

SHAUN GOATER
THE GOAT

HART-BEAST!

Big Johnny Hartson took Gordon Strachan's message to strike fear into the hearts of the opposition a bit too seriously – "Aaarrghhh!".

SAUZEE'S GOOD LIFE!

Not everyone thinks that Scottish football is rubbish. When Franck Sauzee came to play for Hibs, not only did he discover that it's possible to keep up with Celtic and Rangers, but also that life in the highlands is pure joy! **"When I came to Scotland, I had the opportunity to stay for one week, to look at the city and to train with the Hibernian team,"** the former France international told Route 1. **"Hibs wanted to get some new players and I came over, enjoyed the city and the club, and I found a place to stay. That was very important to me because I wanted to continue my career there and I found Scotland very interesting. Edinburgh is a lovely city and I think the Scottish way of life is perfect!"** Calm it down, Franck that's enough – must be the whisky talking again, eh?

TRANSLATING CLAUDIO

WILL SOMEONE TELL US WHAT HE'S GOING ON ABOUT?

BARRY DAVIES: "Claudio, congratulations on the result."
TRANSLATOR: "Claudio, congratulations on the result."
CLAUDIO RANIERI: "Thank you very much."
TRANSLATOR: "Thank you."
BARRY DAVIES: "Claudio, it really looked like the old Chelsea."
TRANSLATOR: "Chelsea looked really old."
CLAUDIO RANIERI: "You're only as old as you feel. They played well."
TRANSLATOR: "I feel they played well, like the team of old."
BARRY DAVIES: "We know you've got players in their 30s, but the way they performed, it could have been a team of youngsters!"
TRANSLATOR: "You have a lot of players in their 30s, but it should have been a team of youngsters out there."

CLAUDIO RANIERI: "Well, I think it's wrong to attack our older players. They are world-class performers and the way they played today shows just that."
TRANSLATOR: "The performance of our older players in attack was world class."
BARRY DAVIES: "I couldn't agree more. A real lesson for any youngsters out there."
TRANSLATOR: "I couldn't agree at all. They would have been shown up by a bunch of children."
CLAUDIO RANIERI: "I'm sick of your insults and this interview is over, you ignorant man."
TRANSLATOR: "I'm sick of your insults and this interview is over, you ignorant man."
BARRY DAVIES: "What?"
TRANSLATOR: "Eh?"
CLAUDIO RANIERI: "Qué?"

WHERE DID IT ALL GO WRONG?

Route 1 dissects the careers of football's great under-achievers!

REFEREES

WHAT THE REFS WERE...

RESPECTED
The referee's word was final. Players did as they were told and rarely talked back. Managers would never speak a word against them.

FEARED
A sending-off was a shameful thing to happen to a player and a club. In that respect, players trod carefully and didn't get involved in any argy-bargy.

CORRECT
Referees didn't have action replays questioning their every decision. So essentially, they were always correct. Just look at the the 1966 World Cup Final and Geoff Hurst's second goal!

INCONSPICUOUS
Referees were known by name and respected. But because their every decision wasn't analysed, they weren't subject to a lot of media attention and were never notorious.

AMATEUR
Refs were schoolmasters from Eton, civil servants, architects and various other professionals. But they refereed out of their love for the game.

WHAT THE REFS ARE...

*******!
We all know the chant about what the ref 'is' but nowadays, that's exactly how they're seen by the fans.

LAUGHED AT
Shoved, intimidated, pressurised, sworn at and abused, referees often carry no real weight with some of today's mega-rich footballers.

INCORRECT
With so many different camera angles, computer-generated tricks and replays, we can check every decision. There are always some that are going to be wrong, but we all see it now.

CONSPICUOUS
Everyone knows about the latest shocking decision and the FA case involving a well-known player or manager. They're now too apparent in today's over-exposed game.

AMATEUR
Refs are schoolmasters from Eton, leisure centre managers, taxi drivers and various other professionals. But they had a big pay rise last year and there are plans to go professional.

WHAT SHOULD THE FA DO ABOUT THIS?
Having professional referees is the only way forward. They'll be fitter, sharper and will earn the money they deserve for their work.

AS GOOD AS IT GETS

Route 1 asks the stars to recall the best of the best from their footy memories.

DENIS IRWIN
MAN. UNITED

FAVOURITE GAME?
"That would be Bayern Munich in the European Cup Final. The way it happened, the way it finished, I can't see anything topping that game at the moment."

FAVOURITE PLAYER?
"John Barnes in the early '90s was one hell of a player for Liverpool, I thought. He got past me plenty of times. He just had everything – he could dribble, he could pass a ball, he was strong and a very good player."

FAVOURITE STADIUM?
"I think the Nou Camp's as good as any. The Bernabeu is a nice little ground as well – not that it's very little! They can all be very intimidating arenas, everything in the Bernabeu's right on top of you; even Valencia have a nice stadium. There are quite a few, Bayern Munich's ground included, but the Nou Camp's massive and it's very special to play in."

BEST TEAM?
"That's hard to say really. Real Madrid are a very good side now. Juventus a few years ago were a very good side as well, so I'd probably pick one of those two."

BEST PLAYER?
"Paul McGrath and Roy Keane are two of the best I've played with, so it's one of those two, but I'm not choosing between them!"

BEST MANAGER?
"I've had a few. I have worked under Jack Charlton, Joe Royle and Alex Ferguson – they're all excellent managers. Obviously I've had the most success under Sir Alex Ferguson, so I suppose I'd have to say him."

BEST TEAM-MATES?
"Well, I think that everybody used to say the 1994 United team was special, but I think the team now is probably just as good and has maybe even surpassed that."

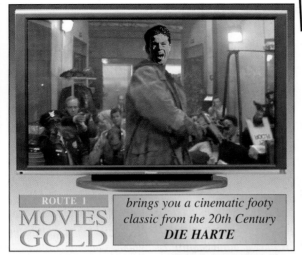

EVERYBODY SINGING VIEIRA'S PRAISES!

Pop along to Highbury and you'll hear Patrick Vieira's name being chanted from almost every corner of the stadium. But it's not just coming from Gunners fans – you'll find Vieira's Arsenal team-mates singing his name as well, as we found out from Robert Pires. **"It's just beautiful to see how much Patrick is loved by the fans,"** Bobi told Route 1. **"When you hear them chanting his name, you feel like singing along."** What about the chant about the referee? You should give that one a go, mate...

FIGO'S ENGLAND ACES!

Who said England have no talented players?

English football lost confidence after Euro 2000, but all we need is a bit of pampering. Route 1 asked Real Madrid star Luis Figo about our best players and he boosted our confidence by picking out Real Madrid co-star Steve McManaman as one of the finest. **"Moving to Spain has turned Macca into an all-round player,"** Figo told Route 1. **"He's moving with confidence and that helps a great talent to shine. There is no doubt he is a great player. In Spain we think he's quality and he can only be a huge asset for England. This kind of talent is needed by every team, but especially at international level when something extra is required to win games. McManaman and Beckham deserve huge respect for their skill. Believe me, England will get there with this kind of player in the team."** That's great Luis, thanks – just don't say any more or our heads will get so big, they'll explode!

PRANKSTERS

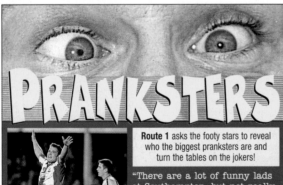

Route 1 asks the footy stars to reveal who the biggest pranksters are and turn the tables on the jokers!

"There are a lot of funny lads at Southampton, but not really any pranksters as such. I do some stupid things, but I don't do anything massive or over the top. I suppose the things we get up to are, like if Hassan Kachloul's got some bad gear on, when he goes out of the dressing rooms we'll tie his shoelaces together and put stuff in his shoes. To be fair though, Hassan does have some pretty bad gear!"

James Beattie
Southampton

CLUB SH

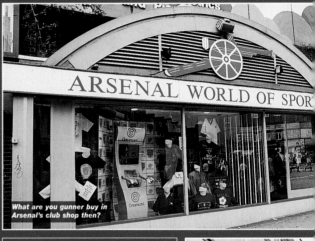

What are you gunner buy in Arsenal's club shop then?

You'll find them at every ground, they're packed every week and sell dozens of multi-coloured wigs. What are they? The traditional footy club shops of course – they're every footy fan's favourite place!

Route 1 decided to pay tribute to the institution that provides fans with all those replica shirts, team mugs and soft toys. But these aren't the only thing they sell. Travel around the UK's club shops and you'll find baby clothes, Scalextric cars, bikes, lanterns, swimming costumes, silly hats, slippers, Monopoly sets and much more. Harrods and Hamleys eat yer hearts out, eh?

In honour of these great retailers, Route 1 did a whistlestop tour of the entire country to show some of the stranger things you can purchase at these fine establishments. There are definitely some weird items on offer in MATCH's club shop round-up!

Posters sell by the dozen down at Southampton FC.

THE CHIPS ARE DOWN!

Welcome to the future of football. No longer will lazy so-and-sos and tubbies be able to drift through games, because the next step in football coaching is almost upon us. Imagine a computer chip in a football shirt or boots which could tell managers about players' heart-rates, speed and skills! This would mean players could be given a genuine rating for every performance and managers could pinpoint those who weren't giving their all during a game! Scientists from Liverpool's John Moores University are trying out their computer chips on Everton and Liverpool, and plans have been made to bring them into the Premiership. Route 1 hopes Matt Le Tissier has retired by the time they're brought in or it could be quite embarrassing!

HELL-BENT ON FOOTBALL!

Blackburn fans should thank their lucky stars that Marcus Bent is bloody-minded. He might be smacking the goals in for Rovers now, but as a teenager Marcus was almost persuaded to take up track and field. Thankfully, his love of football kept him in the game. **"My teachers pushed me towards athletics,"** said Bent. **"They felt my dreams of a career in football were just that and I'd be better off sticking to running. But I had excelled at athletics and by the time Brentford were knocking on my door, I had won a number of trophies. The school's encouragement alerted England and they wanted me to run for them, but I had already set my heart on a career in football and signed YTS forms for Brentford."** And athletics' loss is definitely Blackburn's gain!

OP CRAZY!

THE WEIRD AND WONDERFUL COUNTDOWN!

1 WEST HAM UNDERWEAR

Top support for the ladies! And you can keep your club a secret...

2 ASTON VILLA ARMCHAIR & TEDDY
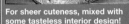
For sheer cuteness, mixed with some tasteless interior design!

3 DERBY RAMS HAT

Can you see yourself walking down the high street with that?

4 SUNDERLAND ARMCHAIR SUITE

How about settling down to watch The Black Cats on one of these?

Hoddle shirts are much sought-after at The Lane.

5 BRADFORD BOOT FRESHENER

Because Bradford City caused a real stink in the Premiership?

6 COVENTRY 'FEZ BOYS' T-SHIRT

A tribute to Hadji and Chippo. They're Moroccan, you know!

7 SPURS DARTBOARD

We're not sure if it comes with a free photo of George Graham!

8 LEEDS UNITED UNDERWEAR

Who needs Calvin Klein when you have the Leeds United version?

9 ARSENAL DOUBLE SOUVENIR

A very cute tribute to Arsenal's fantastic 1997-98 Double season.

10 NEWCASTLE TABLE FOOTBALL

Relive magical Toon moments with this table football game!

GUPPY THE PUPPY

Are you a teenage midget? Do you sometimes feel embarrassed by your lack of size or weight? Do you feel like a wimp? Well Route 1 can't help you. But don't worry – Leicester City winger Steve Guppy once felt exactly the same way, and he went on to play for England! So if you feel like you're a little titch, don't worry because, according to Gupps, growing can come late! **"When I left school I was the second smallest lad in my year,"** admitted Gupps. **"I didn't really shoot up until I was about 18 or 19. With that came a bit of pace and I suppose my confidence grew from there."** Good stuff. Just remember to eat your greens and get lots of sleep and you could play for Wycombe and Leicester too!

HOLD THE BACK PAGE!

How Eriksson could make the headlines!

SING SVEN YOU'RE WINNING!
Congratulations Sven, you've won England the World Cup and the Euro Championships. Keep up the good work, sson!

BECKS IN SVENTH HEAVEN!
The Three Lions beat France 7-0 in the Stade de France, with captain David Beckham scoring all seven of England's goals. Loverly jubberly!

ERIKSSON PHONES HOME!
Rumours that the England manager is homesick are soon quashed when he reveals his love of London.

SWEDE FA!
Super Sven discovers that the FA isn't a soft touch when it refuses him a new, improved £4 million-a-year contract. Cue a massive debate in the media about Eriksson's worth.

ERIKSS-ON YER BIKE!
You've just lost again, Sven. Results better improve soon because the witch hunt is just starting in the tabloid press!

OVER SVEN OUT!
England crash out of the World Cup with a Second Round loss to Romania. The last-minute goal after a slip by Joe Cole sees England leave Japan and Korea early.

SVEN LOVER ERIKSSON!
A sleazy Sunday newspaper makes shocking revelations about the England boss. But are the allegations true? And do we really care about them?

SVENGATE: ERIKSSON SUES US!
Eriksson takes a newspaper to court over allegations of having a secret lovechild. He is eventually handed a hefty £650,000 in an out-of-court settlement with the tabloid.

GORAN GORAN GONE!
Eriksson quits the England job, claiming the pressure was too great, particularly with the intrusion into his personal life. Peter Taylor takes over again.

THIS CHARMING MAN!

Alan Curbishley wastes no time in brushing aside a critic with the kind of dry wit we now expect from the Charlton boss!

ROUTE 1 OPTA

Who's the biggest under-achiever in Premiership football – Tottenham or Everton? Route 1 munches the stats to find who's the bigger fallen great.

	SPURS		EVERTON
	2	League titles	9
	0	Premiership titles	0
	3	European titles before 1990	1
	0	European titles since 1990	0
	7	Managers since 1990	6
	0	Chances of winning the title in 2002	0
	0	Chances of winning the title again	0
	40,000	Dissatisfied fans	40,000
	40,012	**TOTAL**	40,016

CONCLUSION Both of these top-flight teams are sleeping giants, but Everton are the bigger lazy dogs of the two. Time to wake up you Toffees!

NOBBY'S NOT GETTING YER!

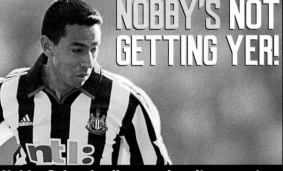

Nobby Solano's all ears when it comes to getting to grips with his Geordie chums in the North East. Well, he has to be really – given their sometimes incomprehensible babblings. While the Nobster was chatting away with Route 1, he told us the problems a Peruvian in the Toon can often have. **"Sometimes when I speak with Geordie people, I find it a little difficult to understand,"** he explained as we nodded sympathetically. **"When I hear people from London or all different kinds of places, I can hear that it's different. It's the same with Scottish players, you know that with players in the team like Kevin Gallacher, sometimes it's, 'Sorry, what are you saying?'"** So being the nice people we are at Route 1, we asked Kevin Gallacher to maybe slow down for Solano. He told us: **"Auch nae, ah cannae see ah cun dee tha' ken."** Hmm, it seems wor Nobby might have a point!

do you remember your
FIRST...

Ipswich Town defender Hermann Hreidarsson strolls down memory lane with MATCH!

...FOOTBALL BOOTS

"My first ever boots were a pair of Patricks that were endorsed by Kevin Keegan! When I was growing up in Iceland Keegan was a popular player. I do remember that the boots were pretty crap and cheap though!"

...PRO GAME

"In England, my first game was for Crystal Palace and it was against Wimbledon. Of course I played for Wimbledon later on, but that was my first game playing against them. No, hang on! I came on as sub for Palace against Blackburn before that, but my first ever start was against Wimbledon!"

...GOAL

"It's funny because in 1994 I scored my first goal in Iceland playing for my team IBV. Eidur Gudjohnsen, who plays for Chelsea now, also scored his first goal in that same game. He was playing for the opposition – a team called Valur."

...GAME AS A FAN

"I don't think I can remember that one. I used to watch a few of the local games as a youngster, but there's no point me telling you the teams because you will have never heard of them!"

...CAR

"Yeah, it was a Ford Sierra – it was really old and crap! I only had that car for six months because it was really thirsty. It just guzzled up the petrol. Then I got a Lada Samara!"

...RED CARD

"I remember one red card well. I got booked and then around two minutes later I went to take a throw, but I didn't realise it wasn't our throw. So I threw the ball away and the referee sent me straight off. I was only ten years old at the time as well!"

MR DISAGREEABLE

You're always wrong with COVENTRY's flame-haired boss.

MRS DISAGREEABLE: "Could you check the time?"
MR DISAGREEABLE: "Och no I cannae agree."
MRS DISAGREEABLE: "Just check the speaking clock for me will you?"
Mr Disagreeable calls the speaking clock...
SPEAKING CLOCK: "At the third stroke the time will be 3.12pm and 50 seconds."
MR DISAGREEABLE: "Och no, I cannae agree."
SPEAKING CLOCK: "At the third stroke the time will be 3.13pm precisely."
MR DISAGREEABLE: "Och no, I cannae agree with tha'. You was speculating on the time last season."
SPEAKING CLOCK: "At the third stroke the time will be 3.13pm and 10 seconds."
MR DISAGREEABLE: "Och no, I cannae agree with tha'. Nobody has time for Coventry City FC, but..."
SPEAKING CLOCK: "At the third stroke the time will be 3.13pm and 20 seconds."
MR DISAGREEABLE: "Och no, I cannae agree. Youse can write of Coventry City FC, but..."
Disagreeable hangs up...
MR DISAGREEABLE: "Och, can yae believe tha'...?"
MRS DISAGREEABLE: "Did you get the time, love?"
MR DISAGREEABLE: "Eh...?"

I'm niver wrong and ye knoo I'm reet aboot tha'!

HARTSON'S DIRTY DENS!

Not many things scare John Hartson. But mention the name 'Dens Park' to him and shivers will go down his spine. Because Dundee's stadium is the venue of his most painful football memory ever – literally! **"Dens Park? I broke my arm there playing for Wales' Under-15s,"** shivered John. **"It's the only time I've ever broken my arm. I fell awkwardly and ended up in the Scottish Royal Infirmary, and I had to travel back for ten hours on the coach. I had a busted arm and they plastered it too tight for me. My fingers were going blue and I had to go straight to hospital when I got back to have it re-plastered. I was in absolute agony! We won 4-0 or 5-0 but I couldn't enjoy the post-match celebrations because I had to go off after two minutes. I'll definitely never forget Dens Park."** Blimey. We reckon John could probably do with seeing a psychologist about that! But not one in Dundee, eh?

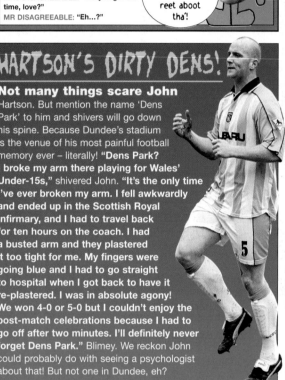

We thought Abel Xavier's look had been done before. Now we know where the Everton star got if from – ancient Pirate Yellowbeard. Grrr!

ABEL SEAMAN!

F.R.I.E.N.D.S

match asks the stars who their best mate in footy is

"My best friend in football is Mark Draper. We played together at Leicester and then Villa. I'm still good friends with Simon Grayson as well, who played for both teams. I still speak to them quite often. Very often, actually!"

• julian joachim •

David Dunn & co. have enjoyed stepping up to the Premiership.

The man in charge of the academy, Bobby Downes.

The chef has a brief to cook up healthy meals.

WASH & GOALS

David Ginola might have been washing his lovely locks with L'Oreal shampoo for a while now 'because he's worth it' – but not all of the Premiership's footy players have been following the Frenchman's fine example. The truth is, there's a rival to the famous L'Oreal brand. Don't get the wrong idea – we haven't been asking all the players about the toiletries they use, but Route 1 can now exclusively reveal that all 20 Premiership clubs have got 'Wash & Go' dispensers in their dressing rooms, allowing the players to literally wash their hair and go! Regular users of 'Wash & Spend Ages Brushing It Down & Putting Gel On It Because It's Gone All Fluffy' in the Nationwide League must be extremely jealous of their top-flight counterparts!

ROVERS ACADEMY LIFE!

Blackburn are back in the Premiership and this time they want to stay there. Rovers may be one of only three sides to have won the Premiership title, but they were criticised for spending a fortune to get there. So before owner Jack Walker died, he made a pledge to leave a lasting platform upon which the club could build its future success – a youth academy which would be the envy of the country. The idea was to have a small site next to the senior team's training ground at Brockhall, with facilities within easy reach, as academy director Bobby Downes explained: **"The indoor sports hall here is the best in Europe. It is half the size of a football pitch and has a special type of astro turf so thick it can take a stud. It has a four-lane sprint track and a TV gantry outside to film the Under-19s; it's also surrounded by woodland and has a running hill."**

One of Rovers' star players, David Dunn, came from the youth team and he took time out to give Route 1 a tour of the academy. **"I'm really impressed and a lot of people are now saying this academy is the best in the country. If you're a 12-year-old and you look at the facilities, you can only be impressed. I would have liked all this when I was young!"** Dunny adds. **"The academy cost £7 million and Damien Duff, who's a former youth player in the first team, is worth that now. If in time the manager wanted to sell a player, then he could make the money back."** So it's watch out Manchester United – Rovers are ready to take your crown of having the best youth system around.

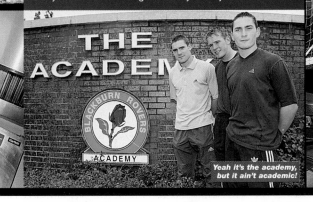
Yeah it's the academy, but it ain't academic!

The Blackburn boys are getting Rovers roaring!

The youth players have their own gym.

Dunny's always been first off the mark...

These lads are proof that the youth set-up works.

This is Europe's best indoor sports hall.

Players use the pool for physiotherapy.

S.O.S

Help us to 'Save O'Neill's Scarf'! MARTIN O'NEILL has lost his Celtic scarf. It's the one with green and white stripes on. Can you spot it?

THE GROWING PAINS OF STEVEN GERRARD, AGE 21 & 1/2

Steven Gerrard is growing into the best all-round midfielder in the country. But it's taking time. The 21-year-old Liverpool and England star has sprung up over the past year, which has caused several niggling injury problems, but Reds' manager Gerard Houllier hopes that, as he gets older, last season's PFA Young Player Of The Year will be able to play games more regularly. **"He's gradually building up his figure,"** explained Houllier.

"At the moment, it's two games out of three. Ideally, it'll become three out of four but you must remember he's still very young. In the space of 12 months he has actually grown considerably – two inches in height and a stone in weight – and that's unusual. When he was a boy, he was very small, so he's obviously different from most."

Let's get this right – he was small as a boy and then he got bigger? Well that's definitely different from most lads, Gerard! Except for Gianfranco Zola and Nick Barmby that is…

NATURE TAKES ITS COURSE WITH PSYCHO!

When it comes to footy dedication, Stuart Pearce is an example to any professional. With a playing career spanning three decades, the defender has shown that players can keep going as long as they want to. But is the man they call 'Psycho' different to the wide-eyed youngster who emerged at Coventry back in 1983? **"Without a doubt,"** he told Route 1. **"The things that I used to do ten years ago I can't do any more. I've got to use my head a little bit more than my legs! But that's part of nature, I'm afraid to say."** Wot, like nutting people instead of kicking them? Only joking, Psycho!

BECKHAM'S

IN THE FIRST GAME OF THE 1996-97 SEASON, Man. United were cruising to a 2-0 victory when their No. 24 received a pass on the halfway line. With a brief look up, he took one casual touch and unleashed a 60-yard arrowed drive towards goal. With the ball dipping, fans arched their necks to follow its flight then leapt from their seats as the ball crashed under the crossbar and into the net. It was the start of a remarkable rise to fame for David Beckham. Five years on, he now boasts five league championship medals and a reputation as one of the finest players in the world.

Even a red card at France '98 failed to halt the midfielder's progress. He inspired United to the treble in 1999 and was named England captain last season – the proudest moment of his career.

Off the field, his high-profile relationship with Victoria Adams has boosted his image to pop star status. Companies queue up for his services, but he remains focused and still harbours a burning desire to become the best footballer in the world.

There is surely more to come from Becks, but he's already written two books about his life and has a fascinating story to tell. MATCH has kept a scrapbook on the Man. United star ever since we interviewed him as a fresh-faced teenager in 1995. Now you can follow the story of how he reached the top with club and country!

▲ A YOUNG BECKS REACHING FOR THE STARS

Ever since he can remember, Becks has played football and as a kid he used to regularly practise in his parents' back garden. As a Manchester United fan, he soon developed the dream to play for them one day and he was even a mascot at a game in London, near where he lived.

When he was 11 years old, Becks went along to the Bobby Charlton Soccer School in his school holidays. He made such an impression that he won a Skills Award, which was presented to him at Old Trafford on a matchday. **"I think I'm still the youngest player, at 11, to win the Soccer School and it was significant because that launched United's initial interest in me,"** said the midfielder. As part of his prize, he was given the chance to watch a live match in Barcelona! **"I won a competition to go to the Nou Camp Stadium in Barcelona to be with stars like Mark Hughes and Gary Lineker,** who were both playing there at the time. It was a really good experience."

Becks was brought up near West Ham's Upton Park and went for trials at Leyton Orient, as well as representing Essex Schoolboys as a youngster.

SCRAPBOOK!

◀ THE UNITED BOY

When he was 16, David's dream came true when he was awarded a trainee contract with United. He travelled north to live in digs, but although he was a long way from home, he soon settled in and made friends with the likes of Gary Neville, Paul Scholes and Nicky Butt. The young group of stars formed the nucleus of a successful youth team and lifted their first of many trophies together when they won the 1992 FA Youth Cup in their first season at Old Trafford.

"I was only ever interested in one club and that was United. I used to train as a kid at Tottenham, but I always wore my Man. United kit."

▶ GETTING FIRST-TEAM ACTION

David was handed his first-team debut by Alex Ferguson in the League Cup against Brighton on October 1, 1992. He had to wait two years for his United league debut, though, and was sent on loan to Preston. **"When Alex Ferguson told me I was going for a loan period at Preston, my first thought was 'What is going on?' but I really enjoyed it. It was a matter of gaining confidence. I played a few games and came back to United buzzing. It made me more determined to see first-team action."**

◀ ENGLAND HONOURS

After playing nine times for England's Under-21 side, Becks was called up by Glenn Hoddle and made his senior debut against Moldova in a 3-0 win. **"It was incredible,"** said Becks. **"I got a buzz from being around stars like Shearer, Gascoigne and Ince. Just playing in the same team as them was incredible."**

"I used to clean the players' changing room in my first year and the boots in my second. Brian McClair used to give me the biggest tip!"

▶ FIRST-TEAM GLORY

After making just four first-team appearances for United in the 1994-95 season, Becks finally got his chance to play regular football in the following campaign and wasted no time showing people what he could do. Even though his preferred role was in the centre or on the right of midfield, he deputised for the injured Ryan Giggs on the left and partnered Andy Cole for an extended spell up front. He went on to score seven goals from 33 games as United won the Premiership and FA Cup double, beating Liverpool 1-0 at Wembley. 'Match Of The Day' pundit Alan Hansen was made to eat his words when Becks and co. lifted the league trophy after he memorably stated earlier in the season, 'You'll never win anything with kids'.

BECKHAM'S Big moments!

1986
David Beckham becomes the youngest player ever to win the Bobby Charlton Soccer School and earns a trip to Barcelona to train with Mark Hughes and Gary Lineker. Man. United express an interest in taking him on as a schoolboy trainee!

1989
David signs associated schoolboy forms with United, meaning he'll be travelling to Manchester on weekends and in the school holidays to train with his new club. While Becks is delighted, his grandad is rather upset because, as a season ticket holder at White Hart Lane, he hoped his grandson would sign for Tottenham, with whom David had been training for the past two years.

JULY 8, 1991
Turning down big-money offers from Spurs, as well as trials with Arsenal and West Ham, Becks signs up for an apprenticeship at Old Trafford.

MAY 1992
In his first year in the United youth team, Becks is part of the side which wins the FA Youth Cup final, beating Crystal Palace 6-3 over two legs. Also in the Manchester United team is best mate Gary Neville, Phil Neville, Nicky Butt and Paul Scholes.

SEPTEMBER 23, 1992
Alex Ferguson calls 17-year-old Beckham into the first-team squad to play away to Brighton in the League Cup. United are winning 1-0 when David comes on as a substitute for Andrei Kanchelskis, but Brighton equalise a minute later.

JANUARY 29, 1993
Even though David's still got a few months left on his apprenticeship at United, boss Alex Ferguson decides he deserves a professional contract!

MAY 1993
David suffers his first taste of defeat as the United youth team are beaten in the final of the FA Cup. The young side loses 4-1 on aggregate to a Leeds side featuring striker Noel Whelan.

MAY 1994
Becks pockets another medal, this time for winning the Pontins Central League title, playing 16 games for United's reserves during 1993-94.

JAN 1995
Alex Ferguson thinks his young prodigy needs first-team experience after impressing in the reserves, so he sends him out on loan to Division Three side Preston North End. Becks is keen to show what he can do and scores two goals in five appearances from midfield, including a brilliant free-kick which is shown on national television.

APRIL 2, 1995
As Manchester United battle it out with Blackburn Rovers for the Premiership title, Becks is given his league debut against Leeds at Old Trafford. He starts the game, but United are disappointed with a 1-1 draw against George Graham's side.

MAY 1996
The midfielder is handed an extended run in the first team in the 1995-96 season, and scoring an impressive seven goals from 33 games helps United to win the Premiership and FA Cup double.

JUNE 1996
While all eyes are focused on the senior squad at Euro '96, Becks is trying to make an impression with England's Under-21s in Toulon. The midfield star captains the side, but they're soon on the plane home after a disappointing tournament.

AUGUST 1996
Beckham makes headlines again at the start of the new season by scoring with a brilliant chip at Wembley as Man. United beat FA Cup runners-up Newcastle United 4-0 in the Charity Shield.

SEPTEMBER 1, 1996
Beckham's good form impresses new England manager Glenn Hoddle and he gets his first senior cap in a World Cup qualifier in Moldova. England win 3-0, but Becks has to wait until February 1997 to play for England at Wembley. Unfortunately, it's not the best result – a 1-0 home defeat to Italy.

CARLING CHAMPIONS

BECKHAM'S SCRAPBOOK!

▼ WONDER GOAL FROM THE HALFWAY LINE

In their opening game of the 1996-97 season, United found themselves beating Wimbledon 2-0 away at Selhurst Park. With just a minute remaining, Becks spotted Dons 'keeper Neil Sullivan off his line and struck a spectacular 60-yard lob that dipped into the back of the net. The goal launched him as a Premiership star and made him a household name. **"I didn't give it a second thought, I just hit it,"** Becks explained. **"I certainly meant to do it. We had already won the game when I spotted the 'keeper off his line and thought I might as well have a go. I was fortunate that I struck it well and it dipped at the right moment. Afterwards, Neil Sullivan congratulated me on a great goal, which was nice of him. I'd tried it in reserve and youth games, but for it to come off in the Premiership was brilliant! I've seen replays, but if I'm honest, you could try that shot 100 times and it would never come off again! It's one of those goals that I will look back on in a few years' time and think, 'Did I really do that?'"**

▼ BEST YOUNG PLAYER

Winning a second league title in a row with United and earning a regular place with England was enough to see Becks voted by his peers as the 1997 PFA Young Player Of The Year. "It took a bit of time to sink in. I felt honoured to get nominated, so to win it was fantastic. You think, 'Do people really think I'm that good?'"

"My parents have always wanted the best for me. My dad has always been a Man. United supporter so he was over the moon when I joined the club."

▲ BECKS THE TREND-SETTER

While Beckham's talent shone through on the pitch, he also became a style icon off the field and was never out of the papers. With a Spice Girl for a girlfriend, as well as attending fashion shoots and glamorous parties, Becks seemed to have a busy life away from football. **"My lifestyle seems to intrigue people. I realise that because my girlfriend Victoria is famous and appears regularly in the newspapers, it gives the wrong impression because people think we're always out socialising. But in truth I spend a great deal of time at home, preparing myself mentally and relaxing between games. I have to work hard at my game, I always have done. I still stay behind after training and I couldn't do all that if all I did was socialise."**

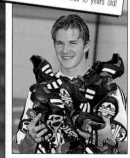

Becks became a Brylcreem boy when he signed a deal to publicise the firm's hair products. He also revealed he'd worn Brylcreem gel since he was 13 years old!

▶ QUALIFYING FOR THE 1998 WORLD CUP

Beckham was selected to play against Italy in the crucial final qualifier in Rome, with England needing a point to go through to the 1998 World Cup. Italy had already beaten England at Wembley, but Hoddle's men drew 0-0 to secure a place in the tournament. **"From the first time I kicked a ball I dreamed about playing at a World Cup,"** said Becks. **"I can't really explain the feeling of joy or relief!"**

▲ THE PREDATOR

After scoring his wonder goal at Wimbledon wearing a pair of Predators, David was quickly snapped up by German manufacturers Adidas and got paid simply for wearing the boots!

When he became a father to Brooklyn in March 1999, Becks felt his life was complete. **"It's the greatest thing that has ever happened to me,"** said Becks. **"I've never been so happy and I think I am content in my private life. Since Brooklyn has come along I feel I've grown up a lot and he's made me look at life from a different perspective."**

The Mirror
DIANA'S BIRTHDAY
Stunning 3 page tribute on the day the world held them 37
10 HEROIC LIONS ONE STUPID BOY

The tabloids gave Becks a hard time after his sending-off contributed to England crashing out at France '98.

▲ BECKS SEES RED AT THE WORLD CUP

David's World Cup dreams turned to tatters when he was red-carded for a retaliatory kick at Diego Simeone of Argentina and ten-man England were knocked out of the tournament. He came home to intense ill-feeling from football fans who blamed him for the early exit. **"I felt terrible, but no matter how many times I said sorry, it didn't make any difference to some people."**

As European Cup winners, United played in the World Club Championship in Tokyo but Becks made the headlines for the wrong reasons with another red card.

▶ THE NEW KING OF EUROPEAN FOOTBALL

Critics and supporters kept talking about it, but whenever they had the chance, Man. United's players would brush aside any thoughts of completing a momentous treble. Only when the end of the 1999 season was in sight did United believe they could add the European Cup to the Premiership and FA Cup in the same season. **"The treble has to be the best mark of my career. I would have played in goal in the European Cup final if it meant I was going to play!"** said Becks. **"There was a great party afterwards, with plenty of soft drinks!"** Beckham's fantastic contribution to United's success in Europe was recognised by UEFA when it awarded him the 1999 Champions League Player Of The Year award, ahead of such luminaries as Barcelona's Rivaldo and Juventus midfielder Zinedine Zidane.

BECKHAM'S Big moments!

AUGUST 1996
On the opening day of the 1995-96 season, with United already winning 2-0 at Wimbledon and with just one minute left to go, Beckham picks up a loose ball on the halfway line and, spotting 'keeper Neil Sullivan off his line, deftly lobs him from 60 yards to score the Goal Of The Season.

OCTOBER 1996
After scoring *that* wonder goal from 60 yards wearing a pair of Adidas Predators, Becks signs a massive six-figure contract to wear the flashy boots permanently for the German manufacturers. The sportswear company acts fast after seeing the potential of the United star, who agrees to publicise all of the firm's football-related products.

MAY 1997
Beckham has a great season with Man. United, winning his second Premiership title. His talents are recognised by his peers when he is named the 1997 PFA Young Player Of The Year. He also comes second to Alan Shearer in the Player Of The Year category, a fine testament to his ability.

AUGUST 1997
As the country starts Becks-mania, Brylcreem also decides to get in on the act and signs up Beckham to endorse its hair products.

OCTOBER 1997
Beckham continues to play an important role in England's bid to qualify for the 1998 World Cup finals under the management of Glenn Hoddle. Travelling to Rome to face Italy in their last game, it looks almost impossible for England, needing to snatch at least a point at the Olympic Stadium, but Becks and co. put in a tremendous defensive performance to come away with a magnificent 0-0 draw and secure their place at France '98.

OCTOBER 1997
Man. United continue their progress in Europe with an impressive 3-2 victory over Juventus in the Champions League group stages. In a thrilling game, with Becks at his influential best, United come back from 1-0 down to seal a famous home win over a side which had reached the previous three finals of the prestigious competition.

MARCH 1998
United make it through to the last eight of the Champions League and there are high hopes when they draw French side Monaco. But, after gaining a 0-0 draw away, United can only draw 1-1 at home and go out on the away goals rule.

MAY 1998
After famously losing to a struggling Barnsley side in the fifth round of the FA Cup, Beckham ends the season empty-handed, with Arsenal winning a Premiership and FA Cup double.

JUNE 1998
Glenn Hoddle selects the midfielder as part of his squad for the World Cup in France, but Beckham is left on the bench for the first two games against Tunisia and Romania. He's recalled for the match against Colombia and scores a brilliant free-kick to put England through to the next stage. But there's massive heartache as he gets sent-off in the second round against Argentina for kicking out at Diego Simeone after being fouled. The red card leaves England battling on with ten men and they agonisingly lose on penalties after extra-time.

AUGUST 1998
As the new Premiership season starts, Beckham faces a torrent of abuse at every away ground he visits with fans blaming him for England's exit from the World Cup. But Becks ignores offers to escape all the verbal abuse with a move abroad and lets his feet do the talking for United.

MARCH 1999
The day after playing against Inter Milan in a Champions League match at Old Trafford, Becks travels down to a private hospital in London where his fiancée, Victoria, gives birth to a baby boy – who they name Brooklyn.

APRIL 1999
Becks scores a magnificent volley against Arsenal in an FA Cup semi-final replay. In what proves to be an epic game at Villa Park, Dennis Bergkamp equalises for The Gunners to make up for an earlier missed penalty. Then in extra-time, Ryan Giggs scores a remarkable individual goal to keep United on course for a possible treble.

MAY 1999
In an extraordinary season, Beckham and his United team-mates first seal the Premiership title with victory over Tottenham on the final day of the season. They then beat Newcastle United 2-0 at Wembley to lift the FA Cup. High on confidence, the team travels to Barcelona to face Bayern Munich in the European Cup final. In the final part of a fairytale treble, the Germans open the scoring and try to defend their lead. United refuse to lie down though. They stage a late comeback with goals from Solskjaer and Sheringham to win 2-1 and are crowned the new kings of Europe.

BECKHAM'S SCRAPBOOK!

Posh and Becks finally got married, but security was so tight that the Press found it hard to get a photograph.

▲ BECKS IS MATCH'S FAVOURITE!

Although Becks didn't quite make the grade as the world's greatest player in 1999, MATCH readers voted him as their Undisputed Player with 35 per cent of the vote, just edging out Arsenal's Kanu. "It really means a lot when football fans, and not just those who support Man. United, appreciate you. I think the fans have been spoilt for choice, so to select me as MATCH's Undisputed Player Of The Year is a great honour."

David Beckham was famed for his highlighted blonde locks, but he shaved them off, then showed his new style to the world by scoring in the next game.

▲ CELEBRATING SUCCESS WITH HIS FAMILY

While he may be a star on and off the pitch, nothing means more to Becks than his family life. In July 1999, he married Victoria Adams at a castle in Ireland, a few months after the birth of their son. The couple sold the photography rights to OK! magazine for £1 million, but it was still the biggest media event of the year, with every newspaper vying to get pictures of the newly-weds. The Beckhams went to the south of France for their honeymoon, but they didn't get much of a break because Alex Ferguson ordered his star midfielder to be back in pre-season training just five days later. It was still the start of a happy life for Beckham, though. "Marriage and fatherhood have both given me responsibilities, but they are responsibilities I love and enjoy. I guess I'm far more patient and I tend to think long and hard about things now. As you get older, you tend to change and have a different perspective on life. I've certainly matured over the last year and I suppose that's down to the way things have changed my life."

Becks went from strength to strength in the year 2000 and critics believed he could go on to become the best footballer in the world one day.

▶ WEMBLEY SORROW

The Football Association decided that the last ever match to be contested at Wembley Stadium would be the World Cup qualifier against Germany. There were high hopes, not only for a good start to the qualifying campaign, but also for a rousing goodbye to the home of football after the win over Germany at Euro 2000. Unfortunately, it wasn't to be and England were beaten by a single goal from Dietmar Hamann. The whole country was in mourning when, after the humiliating defeat, Kevin Keegan resigned from his post as England manager. It left Becks and co. with a qualifier against Finland just days later but with no manager to lead the side. Becks was just as upset as the rest of the team, which went on to draw in Finland.

Becks shared a joke with Juventus star Edgar Davids when they filmed a TV advert for Pepsi. Footballers have a big market value these days!

JULY 1999
It's a big match for Becks as he marries girlfriend Victoria in an Irish castle. Gary Neville is his best man, with other United team mates also present.

NOVEMBER 1999
England finish second behind Sweden in their Euro 2000 qualifying group, so their only chance is the play-offs where they're paired against the auld enemy Scotland. England win 2-0 away, but lose 1-0 at home to reach the Finals.

DECEMBER 2000
It's awards time for Beckham, as his key role in United's treble is recognised when he comes second in the World Player Of The Year rankings behind Brazilian genius Rivaldo. But Becks comes top in the view of our readers when he's voted MATCH's Undisputed Player Of The Year.

JANUARY 2000
Man. United receive an invitation to take part in the World Club Championship in Brazil, which means they opt out of the FA Cup. Despite having high hopes, United find it hard to cope with the hot weather and Beckham is sent-off in a game against Necaxa as United crash out early.

FEBRUARY 2000
After a training ground bust-up, Ferguson leaves Beckham out of the squad to face Leeds. Becks argues that he missed a training session because his son was ill, but his wife is photographed shopping in London that day. Speculation is rife that the feud will result in Beckham leaving, but he's restored to the side for the next game and both parties put the disagreement behind them.

APRIL 2000
After drawing 0-0 away at Real Madrid in the Champions League quarter-finals, United go 3-0 down at home in the return leg. Becks gets them back into the game with a superb solo goal, but his efforts are to no avail as United lose 3-2.

MAY 2000
United beat Aston Villa away on the last day of the season to win the Premiership title by a record 18-point margin, but the players celebrate a week earlier in their last home game against Tottenham. It is an especially proud moment for Becks when he brings his son Brooklyn onto the Old Trafford pitch to parade the Premiership trophy, along with his fellow team-mates and their children.

JUNE 2000
Becks travels to Belgium as a key player in Kevin Keegan's England squad for Euro 2000, but the tournament starts off badly with a 3-2 defeat to Portugal, despite going 2-0 ahead early in the game. Things get better as Beckham supplies the cross from which Alan Shearer scores to beat arch-rivals Germany in the second game, but then it's heartbreak as a last-minute defeat to Romania means England bow out at the first stage.

SEPTEMBER 2000
After the disaster of Euro 2000, the England team has a chance to redeem itself by beating Germany again in a World Cup qualifier. But England put in another below-par performance and lose out to a single goal in the last ever game at Wembley. Kevin Keegan resigns immediately after the game.

OCTOBER 2000
Becks launches his new book 'My World', which features the story of his childhood, career and intimate family life, plus exclusive photography. He's mobbed by thousands of fans at signings in Manchester, London and Dublin, before making an appearance on BBC chat show 'Parkinson'.

NOVEMBER 2000
Peter Taylor, caretaker manager when England play Italy in a friendly, makes Beckham captain. Becks claims it's his 'proudest moment', but he can't help England undeservedly losing 1-0.

JANUARY 2001
Beckham's status as a style icon is recognised when he signs a two-year deal to be the UK face of Police sunglasses for a reported £1 million. United state their desire to win the FA Cup after pulling out of the competition the previous year, but West Ham knock them out at Old Trafford.

FEBRUARY 2001
Speculation is rife over whether Becks will keep the England captain's armband under new boss Sven-Goran Eriksson, but Becks gets the nod in an impressive 3-0 friendly win over Spain.

APRIL 2001
After receiving a booking in the first leg of the Champions League semi-final against Bayern Munich, Becks is suspended for the second leg as United lose 3-1 on aggregate. The team are disappointed and Keane predicts, 'Heads will roll'.

MAY 2001
Becks wins his third Premiership title in a row and it's seven league trophies in nine years for United as they win the championship by ten points.

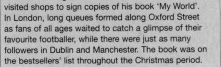

BECKHAMANIA

Newspapers followed Becks on his book tour as the full extent of the public's love for him was shown by the amount of adoring fans who came to see him.

▲ **DAVID TELLS HIS FANS ABOUT HIS WORLD**
Fans across England and Ireland went mad as Becks visited shops to sign copies of his book 'My World'. In London, long queues formed along Oxford Street as fans of all ages waited to catch a glimpse of their favourite footballer, while there were just as many followers in Dublin and Manchester. The book was on the bestsellers' list throughout the Christmas period.

▲ **LEADING OUT THE ENGLAND TEAM**
Becks was chosen by temporary manager Peter Taylor to captain the side in a friendly against Italy. **"The experience was something special for me. It was the proudest moment of my career. Playing for your country is something you always think about as a kid, but going out there as captain of your country is a dream that doesn't happen most of the time."**

◄ **POLICE HELP**
Becks was snapped up to promote Italian-made Police sunglasses as the face of their UK product. **"I like the glasses and as soon as I put them on they felt part of me."**

CAREER CHECK

SVEN GORAN ERIKSSON
England coach

The Swedish coach could be the long-term answer to England's prayers. Route 1 looks at his career so far.

STARTING OUT
Eriksson was born on February 5, 1948. After an undistinguished amateur playing career, he took up coaching with Swedish outfit Degerfors in 1976. **RATING 3**

SWEDE SUCCESS
After a good spell with Degerfors, Sven moved to IFK Gothenburg. He won the Swedish Cup in 1979, and then the treble of league title, cup and UEFA Cup in 1982. **RATING 8**

PORT STAR
Poached by Portuguese giants Benfica after Gothenburg's 1982 glory, Eriksson brought his success with him, winning the league twice, in 1983 and 1984. **RATING 7**

SERIE-OUS SWEDE
Sven moved on to bigger things with Roma in 1984 but found it harder, despite finishing second in Serie A in 1986. He then had a disappointing spell between 1986-88 with Fiorentina. **RATING 4**

BACK TO PORT
Eriksson returned to Portugal with Benfica, reaching the European Cup Final in 1990, only losing to a great AC Milan side 1-0, but won the Portuguese title in 1991. **RATING 5**

SVENDORIA
After his success at Benfica, Sven was enticed back to Italy's Serie A with Sampdoria. However, he achieved little success in five years between 1991-1996. **RATING 5**

SVEN SNUB
Eriksson agreed to take over at Blackburn in June 1997, but he changed his mind when Lazio also showed an interest and joined the Rome club instead. **RATING 4**

EURO CHAMP
Eriksson led Lazio to the UEFA Cup Final in 1998, losing to Inter Milan 3-0. But he guided Lazio to the 1998 Italian Cup and the Cup Winners' Cup Final in 1999. **RATING 9**

TITLE JOY
After a thrilling campaign, Lazio pipped Juventus on the final day of the season for Eriksson to celebrate his first Italian title. **RATING 10**

THREE LIONS JOB
Sven takes over as England coach after a bad run of results at Lazio. He gets off to a great start, winning his first three games, against Spain, Finland and Albania. **RATING 8**

MATCH RATING 6.3
KEEP IT UP SVEN!

AMERICAN BEAUTY

Major League Soccer is attracting some top stars from world football.

America is becoming the new

destination for football stars seeking to earn lucrative contracts at the end of their careers. Germany's Lothar Matthaus, Colombia's Carlos Valderrama and Bulgaria's Hristo Stoichkov have all been big hits in the States, while Paul Gascoigne has made no secret of his desire to end his playing career in the US.

You can't really blame them. The weather's fantastic, particularly in Florida where Martin O'Neill's Celtic usually spend their mid-season break; it certainly helped them last season before returning to capture the Scottish title. The style and pace of the game is slower in America and players aren't mobbed every time they walk down the street as they are in other parts of the world. **"At the end of my career, if I was given the opportunity, I'd love to give it a go,"** Alan Thompson told Route 1 while on Celtic's mid-season break. **"Florida's a lovely place, a fantastic part of the world. I've come here every summer for years."**

It could be a while before we see a galaxy of stars in each Major League Soccer team, but who knows? We may yet see the likes of Dennis Bergkamp, Alan Shearer and Paolo di Canio banging in goals across the Atlantic. But stay clear of those hot dogs lads – you'll have to stay fit to earn your dollars over there!

Valderrama has been a huge hit with the Tampa Bay Mutiny.

Everyone is forced to dress like their captain in the US...

...including the fans, which makes all the games a right laugh!

QUINTON'S INTERNATIONAL IRRITATION

Despite his name, luck doesn't always smile too brightly on Quinton Fortune. The South Africa midfielder is desperate to play for Manchester United but when he's not injured, he's off playing for his country. **"The time away on international duty hasn't helped,"** Fortune groaned to Route 1. **"But since I've been injured and had time to think, I realise you can't make excuses when you're a professional footballer. You have to handle all types of situations at this level. In the past, I got despondent about playing for South Africa and disrupting my progress at United. But I have to accept it."** Good stuff. We suggest you put your efforts into replacing Ryan Giggs and becoming the new wing wizard at Old Trafford.

rio improvement!

Rio Ferdinand continues to improve at Leeds, so Route 1 is left wondering exactly how good he can be! According to the £18 million defender, it's all down to the boss. **"Managers have different ideas. No disrespect to Harry Redknapp, but David O'Leary has been good for me,"** said Rio. **"His record as a defender was one of the main things that drew me here. In becoming the best you must learn from people who have been there and done it, and O'Leary fits into that category."** It's a good job Rio didn't move to Man. United. He would have perfected the art of whinging there!

THE UNNATURAL GAME!

Football seems to be the most natural game in the world, but not if you listen to Professor Football himself, Arsene Wenger! **"Football is something which is not natural,"** said the Arsenal manager, leaving everyone scratching their bonces. **"We're not really built to play football. It takes a lot of concentration, you have to watch the ball and also lift your head to look around you. It takes a lot of practice and encouragement."** Ah, we agree with you entirely now Arsene. You're saying it's about time you encouraged Ray Parlour to practice a bit more, right?

GETTING GOBBY!

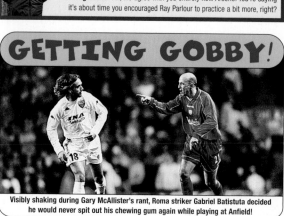
Visibly shaking during Gary McAllister's rant, Roma striker Gabriel Batistuta decided he would never spit out his chewing gum again while playing at Anfield!

Bobby Robbo's CAPITAL PUNISHMENT

Whatever you do, don't send them to that London!

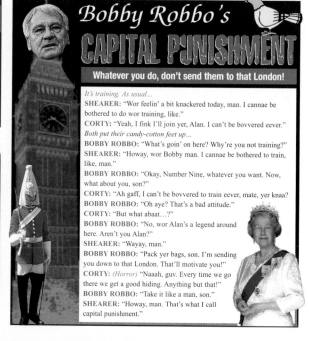

It's training. As usual...

SHEARER: "Wor feelin' a bit knackered today, man. I cannae be bothered to do wor training, like."

CORTY: "Yeah, I fink I'll join yer, Alan. I can't be bovvered eever."

Both put their candy-cotton feet up...

BOBBY ROBBO: "What's goin' on here? Why're you not training?"

SHEARER: "Howay, wor Bobby man. I cannae be bothered to train, like, man."

BOBBY ROBBO: "Okay, Number Nine, whatever you want. Now, what about you, son?"

CORTY: "Ah gaff, I can't be bovvered to train eever, mate, yer knaa?"

BOBBY ROBBO: "Oh aye? That's a bad attitude."

CORTY: "But what abaat...?"

BOBBY ROBBO: "No, wor Alan's a legend around here. Aren't you Alan?"

SHEARER: "Wayay, man."

BOBBY ROBBO: "Pack yer bags, son. I'm sending you down to that London. That'll motivate you!"

CORTY: *(Horror)* "Naaah, guv. Every time we go there we get a good hiding. Anything but that!"

BOBBY ROBBO: "Take it like a man, son."

SHEARER: "Howay, man. That's what I call capital punishment."

THIERRY HENRY
Arsenal

CAPTAIN

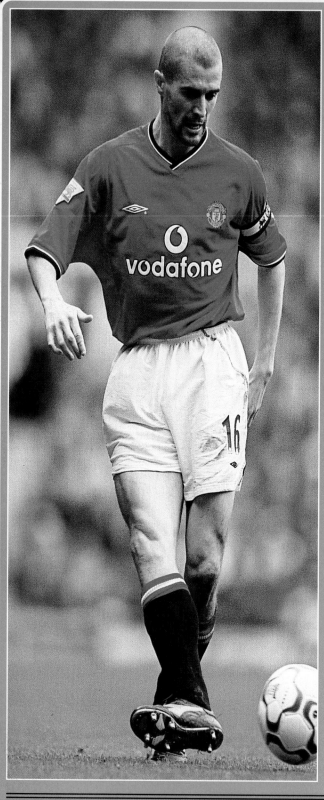

★ **KEANE** ★ **RADEBE** ★ **AD**

Marvels

The Premiership's most inspirational captains tell **MATCH** about the key moments in their illustrious careers.

AT THE HEART OF EVERY SUCCESSFUL TEAM IS a Captain Marvel who leads by example. If things are going well he maintains the momentum. If heads drop it's his job to motivate his colleagues to double their efforts. The skipper knows when to shout and when to give words of advice and it's his ability on the pitch that inspires the rest of the team.

The best captains command respect among their peers by consistently performing at the highest level. They're often chosen at a young age and are more loyal to one club than other players. They might be more open to criticism in defeat but they also get the glory of lifting trophies when things go right – and that's something our Captain Marvels know all about.

Roy Keane has consistently played a leader's role in Man. United's phenomenal success at home and in Europe – a midfield dynamo who is instrumental in breaking down the opposition and setting-up his own team's attacks. Also captain of the Republic Of Ireland, Keane is one of the most passionate players in the game and boasts an enviable trophy cabinet.

In an inexperienced Leeds side, **Lucas Radebe** stands as a commanding presence at the heart of the defence and inspires confidence in those around him. The formidable skipper enthuses commitment and determination for his club and has relished the task of leading South Africa back into world football.

Tony Adams has only ever known one club. His 12-year reign as Arsenal captain has yielded seven trophies and Gunners' fans feel assured when they see the defender's name on the team sheet. A tower of strength and authority, he skippered England to the semi-finals of Euro '96 – the country's best tournament performance in the last decade.

Alan Shearer's mix of power, aggression and proven goalscoring ability has made him a perfect captain for club and country. There is no-one more qualified than the passionate Geordie to lead out the Newcastle side. He wears the armband with pride and has a burning ambition to lift a trophy in front of the adoring Toon Army. Shearer also spent four years as captain of England and led the line with honour against the best teams in the world.

Throughout the annual, our four Captain Marvels explain to **MATCH** what wearing the armband for their club and country means to them. Read on to discover what the skippers have to say about the defining moments in their illustrious careers.

AMS ★ SHEARER ★

CAPTAIN
Marvels

ROY KEANE

> " As a leader, I think it's hard to find anyone to rival him. His commitment and unselfishness are admirable. He drives the team forward and there are so many qualities about him that are overlooked. "

DAVID BECKHAM

ROY KEANE TIMELINE...

AUGUST
MAKING HIS NAME
Launches football career as
a part-time professional after
Cobh Ramblers pip Cork City
for his signature

1986

1987

JUNE
ENGLAND AWAITS
Snapped up by Brian
Clough's Nottingham
Forest for an initial
fee of £20,000

1988

AUGUST
FOREST DEBUT
Makes full debut
for Forest against
Liverpool at Anfield

1989

MAY
WEMBLEY UPSET
Plays for Forest in
FA Cup Final defeat
against Tottenham
IRISH HONOUR
Wins first senior cap
for the Republic Of
Ireland against Chile

1990

MAY
EARLY REWARD
Named Player
Of The Year by
Forest fans

1991

JULY
UNITED AHOY
Agrees verbally to
join Blackburn, but
ends up signing for
Man. United

1992

AUGUST
WINNING START
Makes United debut in Charity
Shield win over Arsenal

1993

ALEX FERGUSON'S PHONE CALL to the Keane family home in Cork one Sunday in 1993 has proved to be one of the most important moments in Man. United's recent history. Keane had returned home to Ireland to think over a move to Blackburn, but his decision was made easy when the United boss invited him to talk about a British record transfer of £3.75 million.

The ex-Nottingham Forest man was the natural choice as captain when Eric Cantona retired from the game in 1997 and he's since become United's pivotal figure in their formidable success at home and in Europe. An inspirational leader and dominant midfielder, the sight of Keane running the length of the pitch to make a last-ditch tackle or score a crucial goal demonstrates not only his athleticism and will to win, but also his unrivalled passion for the game.

MATCH looks at the career of the only captain who could emulate Bryan Robson – Man. United's original Captain Marvel.

ROY KEANE FACTFILE

BORN: August 10, 1971 in Cork

NATIONALITY: Irish

POSITION: Midfield

HEIGHT: 5ft 10ins

WEIGHT: 12st 10lb

FORMER CLUBS: Cobh Ramblers, Nottingham Forest

SIGNED: From Nottingham Forest for £3.75 million on July 22, 1993

MAN. UNITED DEBUT: v Arsenal on August 7, 1993

APPOINTED CAPTAIN: August 1997

TOTAL UNITED GAMES/GOALS: 328/42 (August 1993 to April 2001)

TROPHIES WON AS CAPTAIN: 1997, 1999, 2000, 2001 Premier League, 1999 FA Cup, 1999 World Club Cup

INTERNATIONAL HONOURS: Republic Of Ireland 52/8, Under-21, Youth & Schoolboys

---

JUNE
IRISH ALL-STARS
Plays for Republic Of Ireland in the 1994 World Cup, held in the USA

MAY
SUCCESS STORY
Wins League & FA Cup double with United

1994

MAY
FA CUP UPSET
Lose second successive FA Cup Final to Everton

1995

MARCH
SEEING RED
Captains Republic Of Ireland against Russia – but mars the occasion by being sent-off

1996

MAY
DOUBLE DOUBLE
Helps United to a second Double after FA Cup win over Liverpool

1997

AUGUST
RED DEVILS CAPTAIN
Succeeds Eric Cantona as Man. United captain

MAY
CHAMPIONS AGAIN
Wins third Premiership title with Man. United

1998

SEPTEMBER
INJURY NIGHTMARE
Sustains ligament injury, ruling him out of season

1999

MAY
TREBLE CHAMPIONS
Leads Man. United to an unprecedented treble
WORLD CHAMPIONS
Scores the only goal to win the World Club Cup

2000

MAY
FIFTH TITLE GLORY
Captains United to fifth title in seven seasons and named PFA & Football Writers' Player Of The Year

APRIL
CRITICISES TEAM
Slams United as 'average' after losing to Bayern Munich in the Champions League quarter-finals, but wins Premiership title a month early

2001

1997

AUGUST NAMED MAN. UNITED'S NEW CAPTAIN

Eric Cantona would always be a tough act to follow, but if anyone at Man. United was capable of succeeding him it was Roy Keane. When he arrived at Old Trafford in 1993 he was a quiet newcomer, somewhat in awe of senior players such as Mark Hughes, Paul Ince and Bryan Robson. But by 1997, Keane was more than ready to lead United to even greater levels of success and he took on the captain's armband with immense pride.

"There were a few lads in the running at the time. Gary Pallister was still at the club, as well as Peter Schmeichel and Denis Irwin, but the gaffer decided to go for me. There's a lot that goes with being the captain. When you're skipper of a big club like Man. United there is a lot of off-the-field stuff – like a lot of charities to be involved with. There's also more dealings with the media, and I've had to do all of that because I'm captain of the team. That's a little downside, but the rest are all ups. But as long as I'm winning trophies it doesn't matter, and it doesn't matter who picks the trophies up either – I really mean that."

1997

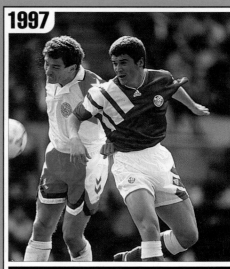

SEPTEMBER LEADING OUT THE REPUBLIC OF IRELAND

Under Jack Charlton, Keane broke into the Republic Of Ireland set-up and soon became a key player in the team's workmanlike midfield, impressing in the 1994 World Cup in the USA. He was rewarded when Charlton stepped aside and Mick McCarthy took over as manager. McCarthy immediately made Keane his skipper, and though injury problems disrupted his run in the side, it wasn't long before he wore the captain's armband again with pride.

"I've a lot of responsibility as Ireland skipper. I've been in the team for quite a long time and there's a lot of good young players coming through now, such as Robbie Keane, Richard Dunne and Damien Duff. The team's changed a lot since I first broke through. But what we need now is to qualify for a big tournament – some of the players need that kind of experience. I played in 1994 and it was fantastic, so these players really need to play in something like a World Cup to step up to another level."

1998

JULY MAKING A TRIUMPHANT RETURN FROM INJURY

Keane suffered the first major setback of his career in September 1997 when his challenge on Leeds midfielder Alfie Haaland left him with a tear to his cruciate knee ligament. It was a serious blow to the Irishman – and Arsenal took full advantage, winning the 1998 Premiership in his absence. But a period of determined rehabilitation helped him to make a playing comeback in United's pre-season tour. It had been a difficult time for the skipper, who'd admitted to being concerned about getting back to his best.

"I'd be lying if I said I got through it quite easily. When I first started coming back it took me a while. Obviously I was going to be a little bit rusty. I always thought it would take a couple of months to get my sharpness back but generally, when I did return, I felt good. There's probably always going to be that thought at the back of your mind that you might not be the same player."

1999

MAY TACKLING THE TREBLE...

The Man. United players tried to dismiss talk of winning the 1999 treble of Premiership, FA Cup and European Cup. But as the months passed and United kept winning, the impossible began to look possible. Keane was at his inspirational best, leading the team to the league title and two major cup finals. He played a key role in the Champions League semi-final win over Juventus to help United to the final, where they beat Bayern Munich to silence the critics.

"People are always talking about the great United teams of the '60s and it's shoved down our throats every week. It wasn't just to shut them up, for our own pride we wanted to win the European Cup – for the manager, the fans, everybody. For me, it's like any trophy, I want to win everything. I want to win the league as much as the European Cup. I mean it – they're both important to me, as is the FA Cup."

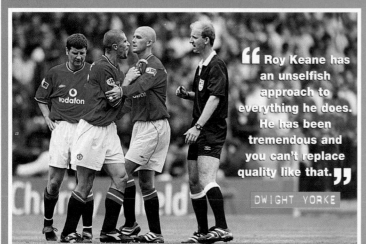

> **Roy Keane has an unselfish approach to everything he does. He has been tremendous and you can't replace quality like that.**
>
> DWIGHT YORKE

1999

MAY ...BUT MISSING OUT ON THE BIGGEST ONE OF THE YEAR

A captain's role doesn't always mean taking centre stage, and Keane was forced to watch from the sidelines for United's finest moment. He limped off injured after just eight minutes of the 1999 FA Cup Final and was suspended for the Champions League Final.

"I was disappointed to get injured, but if I'd been told I'd get a winners' medal before the game, I would have settled for that. I was confident, I knew if we played anywhere near our best we'd win comfortably. And if I'd played in the European Cup Final I'd have had the same desire to get back. People have said to me, 'You missed out,' but that's life. I've been very fortunate in football. You always have your ups and downs and that was just a down for me personally, but for the club, the players, supporters and staff it was fantastic."

1999

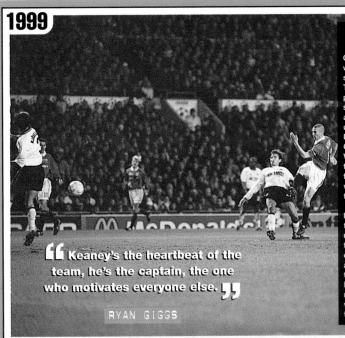

> **Keaney's the heartbeat of the team, he's the captain, the one who motivates everyone else.**
>
> RYAN GIGGS

DECEMBER PLEDGING HIS FUTURE TO MAN. UNITED

Clubs around the world watched with considerable interest as the speculation about Keane's Old Trafford future reached fever pitch at the end of 1999. With six months left on his contract, a host of top clubs were queuing up to snatch him away – but on December 8, the day of United's Champions League clash with Valencia, United announced that their skipper had signed a new four-year deal. As if to prove his worth, Keane crashed home the first goal in United's 3-0 win.

"It was all a bit of a burden. I was patient about it and said that I wouldn't sign a contract until I was ready and the club, to their credit, came up with a contract I felt I deserved. I had always said, right from the start, that my priority was to stay at Man. United and hopefully I can repay the manager and the fans with some more silverware over the coming years."

1999

NOVEMBER MAKING UNITED KINGS OF THE WORLD

United may have conquered Europe in the Champions League, but ruling the world in club football had always eluded British sides until The Red Devils beat Palmeiras in November 1999. United travelled to Tokyo to face the Brazilians in the World Club Cup and it was Keane who bagged the only goal of the game to round off a glorious year for Alex Ferguson's side.

"I was actually relieved to score the winning goal in the end, because I nearly didn't connect properly with the ball to get the touch I wanted. I think it would have been a long journey back to Manchester from Tokyo if we hadn't won the match!"

2000

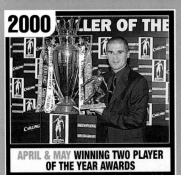

APRIL & MAY WINNING TWO PLAYER OF THE YEAR AWARDS

Keane has never been a player to place a high importance on winning individual awards, but in 2000 – after another year of proving his value to United's relentless pursuit for every honour at home and abroad – he was bestowed with acclaim. First, his fellow professionals voted him the PFA Player Of The Year. The Press echoed those sentiments – naming him the Football Writers' Player Of The Year. The Man. United skipper might have been flattered, but he didn't get carried away with the attention.

"It was a fantastic honour – I never thought I'd see the day when I would be given such an accolade. I was very excited, but you have to see it as a reflection on the whole of the team at Manchester United. I felt very proud and I'm sure my family shared in that too."

2001

APRIL LIFTING A RECORD SEVENTH TITLE WITH UNITED

It may have been a disappointing season in the cup competitions, but no-one could touch United in the Premiership as they raced into an impressive early lead at the top of the table. They were confirmed as champions again in April when Arsenal lost 3-0 to Middlesbrough at home – which seemed to sum up the lack of competition in the Premiership. It was the club's third successive league title and Keane's fourth as captain of The Red Devils.

"Our priority is always to win the league but I think you have to take it one game at a time. I just want that medal in my hand – whether it's with two weeks to go or after the last match. Yes, it's nice to win it early and if we could win it at Christmas, I'd be very happy!"

16

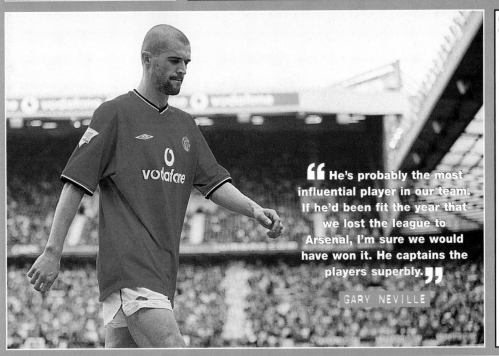

> **He's probably the most influential player in our team. If he'd been fit the year that we lost the league to Arsenal, I'm sure we would have won it. He captains the players superbly.**
>
> GARY NEVILLE

2001

2001-02 STRIVING TO BECOME A UNITED LEGEND

Keane has surely established himself as one of the Manchester United legends in over eight years at Old Trafford. As a midfielder with few equals in world football, he's been one of the team's most valuable players and an inspirational figure for everyone connected with the club. But it would be wrong for Keane to look back on what he's done – he still thinks there's plenty to be won.

"I'd like to be remembered in another four or five years time as a great at United, but I know there's a lot of hard work to do yet. I've had a decent spell at United but I'd like to finish after another few years at the club and be remembered as one of the greats. I think that's every player's ambition, but that's easier said than done."

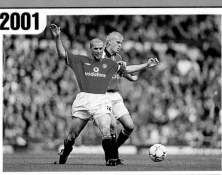

THE FINAL WHISTLE

HOW DID YOU SCORE?
Think you're a footy nut? Check out the questions over the course of the annual and record your answers in the chart on page 106. There's a point for each answer.

Go gunning for glory with these Highbury teasers!

first XI

The Gunners are the biggest club in London, but just how much do you really know about the Highbury outfit?

1 Arsenal famously won the 1989 title on the last day of the season. Which team did they beat 2-0 and who scored the second goal?

2 Ian Wright was one of the most popular strikers to play for The Gunners. When did he move to Highbury and from which club did he leave?

3 Arsenal won the FA Cup back in 1993, but it took a replay and extra-time to clinch the trophy. Which side were they playing against?

4 Which current Premiership manager holds the record for playing the most league games for The Gunners?

5 Arsenal won the European Cup-Winners' Cup in 1994. Which Italian side did they beat 1-0 in the final?

6 George Graham departed Highbury in 1995. Can you name the two top-flight clubs he's left since then?

7 England goalkeeper David Seaman has been with Arsenal since 1990. Which Scottish star's penalty did he famously save in Euro '96?

8 Arsene Wenger took over the manager's position at Arsenal in September 1996. Who did he replace?

9 Hero-turned-villain Nicolas Anelka left Arsenal for Real Madrid in August 1999. How much did the Spanish giants pay for his services?

10 Emmanuel Petit and Marc Overmars made a surprise exit from Highbury last summer. Which leading European club did they join?

11 True or false? Striker Thierry Henry was named the Man Of The Match when France won the Euro 2000 Final in Rotterdam.

THE MEGA WORD SPOT

Can you name the England stars of past and present in the grid below?

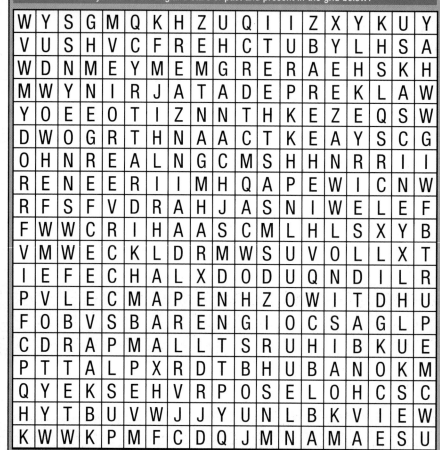

W	Y	S	G	M	Q	K	H	Z	U	Q	I	I	Z	X	Y	K	U	Y
V	U	S	H	V	C	F	R	E	H	C	T	U	B	Y	L	H	S	A
W	D	N	M	E	Y	M	E	M	G	R	E	R	A	E	H	S	K	H
M	W	Y	N	I	R	J	A	T	A	D	E	P	R	E	K	L	A	W
Y	O	E	E	O	T	I	Z	N	N	T	H	K	E	Z	E	Q	S	W
D	W	O	G	R	T	H	N	A	A	C	T	K	E	A	Y	S	C	G
O	H	N	R	E	A	L	N	G	C	M	S	H	H	N	R	R	I	I
R	E	N	E	E	R	I	I	M	H	Q	A	P	E	W	I	C	N	W
R	F	S	F	V	D	R	A	H	J	A	S	N	I	W	E	L	E	F
F	W	W	C	R	I	H	A	A	S	C	M	L	H	L	S	X	Y	B
V	M	W	E	C	K	L	D	R	M	W	S	U	V	O	L	L	X	T
I	E	F	E	C	H	A	L	X	D	O	D	U	Q	N	D	I	L	R
P	V	L	E	C	M	A	P	E	N	H	Z	O	W	I	T	D	H	U
F	O	B	V	S	B	A	R	E	N	G	I	O	C	S	A	G	L	P
C	D	R	A	P	M	A	L	L	T	S	R	U	H	I	B	K	U	E
P	T	T	A	L	P	X	R	D	T	B	H	U	B	A	N	O	K	M
Q	Y	E	K	S	E	H	V	R	P	O	S	E	L	O	H	C	S	C
H	Y	T	B	U	V	W	J	J	Y	U	N	L	B	K	V	I	E	W
K	W	W	K	P	M	F	C	D	Q	J	M	N	A	M	A	E	S	U

- ADAMS
- BALL
- BARRY
- BECKHAM
- BROWN
- BUTCHER
- CHARLTON
- COLE
- DYER
- FERDINAND
- GASCOIGNE
- GERRARD
- HESKEY
- HODDLE
- HURST
- INCE
- LAMPARD
- LINEKER
- MCMANAMAN
- MATTHEWS
- MOORE
- NEVILLE
- OWEN
- PEARCE
- PHILLIPS
- PLATT
- SCHOLES
- SEAMAN
- SHEARER
- SHERINGHAM
- SHILTON
- SMITH
- WALKER
- WILSON
- WISE

MATCHfacts

CODE BREAKER

CAN YOU SOLVE IT?

To keep his starting XI secret, a football manager has coded the name of his star player. The letters have been turned into numbers, but can you work out who this player is? He could play for any team covered by MATCHfacts.

CRACK THE CODE!

23	8	23	10

15	4	1	23	14	1	14

THE PLAYER IS...

	E		E	

SAY WHAT?

Which striker was Peter Ridsdale talking about here?

There's more chance of us signing Father Christmas!

1 POINT FOR CORRECT ANSWER

WHO AM I?

Can you guess the name of this famous player from these statements?

1 I was born in Wallsend, North Shields in 1981.

2 I've come through a highly regarded youth set-up.

3 I've been on loan twice.

4 I'm a promising England midfielder like my mate, Joe.

1 POINT FOR CORRECT ANSWER

CIVVY STREET

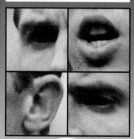

Can you name this top footy star without his kit on?

WHO PLAYS WHERE?

Can you match up these lower division clubs with their grounds?

1. Oldham Athletic	A. London Road
2. Bristol Rovers	B. Griffin Park
3. Peterborough United	C. Boundary Park
4. Wrexham	D. Memorial Stadium
5. Brentford	E. Racecourse Ground
6. Hartlepool United	F. Sincil Bank
7. Lincoln City	G. Ninian Park
8. Cardiff City	H. Underhill
9. Barnet	I. Victoria Park

MATCH
ENTERTAINERS

JOE COLE
England

IN THE DRES

Premiership stars reveal to **MATCH** what it's really like to be in the dressing room.

It's the players who make up the atmosphere – thankfully!

EVER WONDERED WHAT THE PLAYERS ARE doing while you're making your way to the big match or settling down at home to watch a live game on TV? Well, you're about to find out!

The away team eat a healthy, energy-boosting meal at their nearby hotel before arriving at the stadium about an hour before kick-off. The home team arrives slightly earlier to check on injuries, while both sides drink plenty of fluids to prevent dehydration during the game. After the players have had a massage, changed into their kit and warmed-up on the pitch, the manager gives his traditional pre-match team talk – explaining the tactics and what he expects from each member of the side – and then the captain gets his team mates psyched up for the big kick-off.

With an intriguing combination of characters and nationalities, every dressing room is bound to be different, but there are always a couple of players who are louder than everyone else, practical jokers who just never know when to stop messing around, and arguments about what type of music should be blaring out of the stereo!

Now you can find out for yourself, as a host of Premiership stars tell MATCH what really goes on in dressing rooms around the country!

This is where Darren Anderton and co. have their post-match bath.

SING ROOM!

KEVIN PHILLIPS
SUNDERLAND

WHO'S THE LOUDEST IN THE DRESSING ROOM? "Well there are a few actually. We have a good team morale, so we don't just have one or two personalities, the team is equal. We have Don Hutchison who is very lively and gets the lads going, but there's also Niall Quinn, Alex Rae and Micky Gray."

ARE THERE ANY PRACTICAL JOKERS? "We all play jokes and have a laugh, and that definitely rubs off on what we're doing out on the pitch. The masseur is the club's main joker. If someone comes into the changing room when he's doing a massage and asks for the gaffer he'll say, 'Through that door, but make sure you knock first'. Some people have stood there knocking for ages, only to open the door and find out it's a cupboard!"

WHO PLAYS THE MUSIC? "We play music before games, but not before training in the dressing room. We've had the same CD on for the last three and a half years I think, so all the lads know the words off by heart! It's dance music, but I think someone's going to have to come up with a new one soon!"

WHAT'S THE PRE-MATCH TALK LIKE? "Peter Reid doesn't say a lot, to be honest. Our coach Bobby Saxton does more of the talking and the manager comes in five or ten minutes before kick-off and says his piece. He doesn't need to say a lot to us normally, but when he does have something to say all of us definitely listen to him."

JON HARLEY
CHELSEA

WHO'S THE LOUDEST IN THE DRESSING ROOM? "Probably the loudest person was Emmo, Emerson Thome, before he moved to Sunderland a while ago. Apparently Michael Duberry was very loud when he was here, but that was before I started playing in the first team so I don't know. Gus Poyet never stopped talking last season, but the loudest bloke in the dressing room at Chelsea now is Jimmy Floyd Hasselbaink – he just can't talk normally, he has to shout all the time!"

ARE THERE ANY PRACTICAL JOKERS? "Well Graeme Le Saux thinks out some pretty impressive jokes to be honest – he's clever like that – but I suppose our captain, Wisey, does most of the practical jokes, with Jody Morris backing him up all the time as well."

WHO PLAYS THE MUSIC? "No-one, we don't have music in our dressing room any more. We did for a bit – Aaron our kit man used to bring in his little stereo system and pump out some music, but we don't listen to anything now. There would probably be a bad selection of music tastes between us anyway – a lot of dodgy European stuff!"

WHAT'S THE PRE-MATCH TALK LIKE? "It's similar to what it used to be actually. Last season Gus Poyet was translating for the manager, but because he couldn't stop talking he probably added his own stuff onto the end of it as well! The manager is learning English all the time, so that helps."

ASHLEY COLE
ARSENAL

WHO'S THE LOUDEST IN THE DRESSING ROOM? "Probably Patrick Vieira. He's the mouthy one. He's not quiet at all, like his public persona seems. Everyone's loud before a game but Patrick's probably the loudest."

ARE THERE ANY PRACTICAL JOKERS? "That's probably Martin Keown or Dennis Bergkamp. They're always playing pranks! They're funny and our coach, Boro Pirowac, is bad. He's always putting things between his fingers and trying to shake your hand so you hurt your fingers! Boro's a big joker."

WHO PLAYS THE MUSIC? "When Paolo Vernazza was at Arsenal, it was always me and him. But he's gone to Watford now so it's the kit man – the older players didn't like it when we put on some garage stuff!"

WHAT'S THE PRE-MATCH TALK LIKE? "We're just focusing on the game. The boss is always putting confidence in the team and obviously that's good for us. Tony Adams is always loud before the game starts because he's the club captain, but all of the players are loud because we're all up for it."

CLAUS JENSEN
CHARLTON ATHLETIC

WHO'S THE LOUDEST IN THE DRESSING ROOM? I don't know if they'll be unhappy that I told you this! The loudest are probably Chris Powell and John Robinson. They've both been at the club a while and they get all the players going before the games."

ARE THERE ANY PRACTICAL JOKERS? "There are a few jokers and lots of jokes are being played all the time by the players who have been at the club for a few years. It is really good to have a fun atmosphere in our changing room, and part of the fun is having lots of jokes played on you as well."

WHO PLAYS THE MUSIC? "I think Chris Powell decides what music we're going to have playing before the game. We have a lot of soul and R'n'B, and it's nice to have some music on to make us relax. But nobody else gets a chance to bring in anything different!"

WHAT'S THE PRE-MATCH TALK LIKE? "Alan Curbishley is always very prepared and thorough before a game. He knows exactly how other teams play and how we should play to stop them. He gives good team talks!"

DEAN RICHARDS
SOUTHAMPTON

WHO'S THE LOUDEST IN THE DRESSING ROOM? "Hassan Kachloul was loud when he was here. He rarely had his mouth shut, but he's still a funny character! And then there's Beats, James Beattie, who is just incredibly hyperactive when he's off the pitch."

ARE THERE ANY PRACTICAL JOKERS? "There isn't anyone really. We do have a good laugh though – a lot of us take the mickey out of the Norwegians here and how they dress. But I haven't cut up anyone's clothes yet!"

WHO PLAYS THE MUSIC? "It's quite well known that the guys from Artful Dodger are from Southampton and Pete from the band is good friends with a couple of the lads here, Matthew Oakley and James Beattie. He puts together a few CDs for us to listen to in the dressing room before games. I've also done some CDs before. I don't DJ or anything, but I've got some CD mixers at home."

WHAT'S THE PRE-MATCH TALK LIKE? "The manager makes sure that everyone knows what job they have to do, right down to the set-pieces. He gets us organised."

The players will often have massages before a game to loosen up their muscles.

MUZZY IZZET
LEICESTER CITY

WHO'S THE LOUDEST IN THE DRESSING ROOM? "There's not just one person really, but the atmosphere is good, to be honest. We've got a lot of young lads here and a lot of banter, so it's a decent atmosphere."

ARE THERE ANY PRACTICAL JOKERS? "If you come in with bad gear on it ends up in the ceiling! We've got this old ceiling which you can push up and hang clothes from. So you've got to come in decently dressed! For some reason, Matt Elliott's dress sense has improved, so he seems to take the mick more now and put everyone's gear in the ceiling!"

WHO PLAYS THE MUSIC? "We always have music playing before a game. Trevor Benjamin often brings some dance stuff in, but I think Matty Elliott would prefer to have Billy Joel really – he's old school isn't he? There are always arguments about it, some of us like slower stuff, while others prefer dance."

WHAT'S THE PRE-MATCH TALK LIKE? "Peter Taylor normally does the pre-match talk – he gets everyone motivated. After that everyone else starts geeing each other up."

SEAN DAVIS
FULHAM

WHO'S THE LOUDEST IN THE DRESSING ROOM? "I don't think there's anybody who's particularly loud, but it's always lively in the dressing room. It's all very well being hyper, but if you can't take that onto the pitch and win it doesn't mean anything."

ARE THERE ANY PRACTICAL JOKERS? "Again, there isn't really a practical joker, but there's a lot of banter going on in the dressing room. Chris Coleman, who is a really strong character, and Lee Clark do the most jokes."

WHO PLAYS THE MUSIC? "Louis Saha will sometimes bring music in – he's into hip hop and R'n'B. But the trainer at Fulham makes us listen to Country & Western which doesn't go down very well! We've got an American goalkeeper, Marcus Hahnemann, who's made a CD using a mixture of Country & Western and R'n'B stuff, but that's even worse!"

WHAT'S THE PRE-MATCH TALK LIKE? "Jean Tigana does the talk. We'll also sit and watch videos of who we're playing or analyse them on the computer equipment. It's a good atmosphere and everyone tries to stay calm."

GARETH BARRY
ASTON VILLA

WHO'S THE LOUDEST IN THE DRESSING ROOM? "Well, David James probably has the loudest voice! When Gareth Southgate was captain, he always went around to everyone individually making sure they were all right."

ARE THERE ANY PRACTICAL JOKERS? "Ian Taylor's the biggest joker at Villa, he's well known for hanging people's clothes up from the ceiling. It's only the players' dodgy gear he hangs up though – that's his trick!"

WHO PLAYS THE MUSIC? "We never have music playing in our dressing room. I don't know if that's just John Gregory's preference or a club thing, because I've only ever played under one manager at Aston Villa."

WHAT'S THE PRE-MATCH TALK LIKE? "The manager isn't one for ranting or raving before a match. He just gets all the players prepared individually so we all know what we have to do during the game. He's very passionate and tells us what he's thinking. He has a drawing board which he uses all the time – drawing arrows and showing us where he wants us to make runs."

STEPHEN CALDWELL
NEWCASTLE UNITED

WHO'S THE LOUDEST IN THE DRESSING ROOM? "I would say Alan Shearer's the loudest player at Newcastle. You wouldn't think so, but he's always shouting, mucking about and winding everybody up. Him and Rob Lee are the life and soul of the party!"

ARE THERE ANY PRACTICAL JOKERS? "Alan Shearer and Rob Lee again – they're always up to something. Not like me, I'm one of the quiet ones! They do some stupid things like nicking people's socks, cutting them up and hiding your shoes – silly stuff!"

WHO PLAYS THE MUSIC? "We have dance music on in the dressing room – compilation CDs that people bring in – so it's usually quite loud. Me and Speedo, Gary Speed, will often bring in some rock music too – like U2, Oasis and the Rolling Stones to add a bit of class!"

WHAT'S THE PRE-MATCH TALK LIKE? "The gaffer does the team talk at the hotel, then we go over small bits at the ground. He's very animated, he gesticulates and really gees everybody up. He's not a tirant, but he knows what to say to get players going."

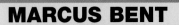

MARCUS BENT
BLACKBURN ROVERS

WHO'S THE LOUDEST IN THE DRESSING ROOM? "That would be Craig Hignett. He's about 32 I think – no, say I said 39! Yeah, he's 39 years old but he runs around like he's 21. He's always playing games even though he's got two kids at home. It amazes me how he gets the energy to look after his kids and still come to training feeling on top of the world!"

ARE THERE ANY PRACTICAL JOKERS? "Probably Alan Mahon. He's come here via Tranmere and Sporting Lisbon. The lads love him and he's always joking around. He's fitted in quickly and the atmosphere is really good."

WHO PLAYS THE MUSIC? "That would be Gary Flitcroft – he plays a lot of house and garage so I quite like his musical taste. The other lads like floppy-hair music, er… indie, but I prefer the more upbeat kind of stuff."

WHAT'S THE PRE-MATCH TALK LIKE? "Graeme Souness basically tells us what it means to us and the club, and tells us to play as a team and give 100 per cent. He gives us confidence and we know we're good enough to compete against the best after his talks."

MARCUS STEWART
IPSWICH TOWN

WHO'S THE LOUDEST IN THE DRESSING ROOM? "That's easy, Jim Magilton! Any of the players will tell you that! He's well known for being loud – he's always going on about something or winding the other lads up with his Irish sense of humour. He's a top bloke though, so we let him get away with it!"

ARE THERE ANY PRACTICAL JOKERS? "Erm, I don't think anyone stands out. Jim likes a laugh, but so do all the lads. Actually, me and Johnno, David Johnson, used to play jokes on each other all the time. When he left to go to Nottingham Forest, I filled his boots with Vaseline. I hope he saw the funny side!"

WHO PLAYS THE MUSIC? "We don't really play any music, but we sometimes have the local radio on. Apparently Kieron Dyer used to play his music before the games, but a few of the others weren't too sure about his taste!"

WHAT'S THE PRE-MATCH TALK LIKE? "I imagine it's pretty similar to others. No-one goes around banging on the walls! The gaffer will run through some things with us and then Matty Holland will maybe say a few words."

RORY DELAP
DERBY COUNTY

WHO'S THE LOUDEST IN THE DRESSING ROOM? "That's definitely Darryl Powell. He's always shouting and being the loudest person in the room – even if everyone's just talking normally. We used to tell him to shut up, but now we just leave him to get on with it!"

ARE THERE ANY PRACTICAL JOKERS? "Stevie Elliot is terrible. He's always up to something. It's usually just stupid stuff, like he'll tape all the cupboard doors shut, or fill them with stuff so it falls out all over you!"

WHO PLAYS THE MUSIC? "We don't have music on any more. A lot of the lads were into rap, but others preferred bands like Oasis, so they'd complain and bring their own stuff in. No-one could ever agree and we were always arguing but Jim Smith got a bit fed up with it all, so we stopped having music altogether!"

WHAT'S THE PRE-MATCH TALK LIKE? "Jim Smith usually has a talk to us and then Colin Todd says something as well. They both focus on tactics and go over set-pieces rather than getting everyone going. Then Darryl will have a word to gee people up for the game."

The Contenders

Route 1 takes a look at the footy players who could follow Vinnie Jones into the movies.

FRANK LEBOEUF
supporting actor

The Frenchman often throws tantrums and loves being the centre of attention, so he'd make a great actor!

ALAN SHEARER
hired extra

The Geordie played a cameo in 'The Match', a rather dodgy footy film, but if he ever fails as a manager…

ALLY McCOIST
on-screen regular

The Scot has already appeared in Robert Duvall's football film 'The Game' and is often on TV shows.

IAN HARTE
stuntman

The Leeds defender has been criticised for diving in the past, so his drama could lead to a big-screen role!

DAVID BECKHAM
big-money star

He's done just about everything else and his wife Victoria was in the Spice Girls film. Watch this space!

JAMIE REDKNAPP
leading man

Jamie and Louise could do a 'Cruise-Kidman' style thriller and they've got the looks to carry it off!

ABEL XAVIER
baddie

With his dyed blonde hair and beard, the Portuguese star looks good for a part in the sequel to 'The X-Men'!

GIOVANE ELBER
romantic lead

Bayern Munich's Brazilian star often bares all in weird photo shoots, making him an ideal film star!

PAOLO DI CANIO
oscar winner

An entertainer on and off the pitch, Di Canio has always said he wants to play himself in a film about his life!

PAUL GASCOIGNE
comedian

Gazza has always acted the clown and loves entertaining his public, so he could be the next Steve Martin!

ROUTE 1 PROGRAMME NOTES!
MATCH REVEALS WHAT THE PROGRAMMES REALLY SAY!

DAVID O'LEARY *writes*

Hello there and a big welcome to today's clash with the mighty Ipswich Town. And who would believe it? My lads playing against the likes of Ipswich in the Premiership? It's a wonderful occasion for us to have a club as prestigious as Ipswich playing at Elland Road, so it is. To be sure, we've got a good young side here and I just want the lads to go out there and enjoy the game and do their very best. But they're all just babies, so they are, and with all the injuries we've suffered – two of our reserve team players are both suffering from minor knocks for today's game – to get a result from this match would be an amazing achievement for little Leeds United.

Not that I'm making excuses now, loyal supporters, but I'm already expecting some really shocking refereeing decisions this afternoon. And of course I'm a young naive manager who is just learning his trade in the game. Again, as long as my lads just run around with their heads held high and respect themselves and the referee, that's all that matters. And if we win, by some miracle, we won't get carried away and think we could possibly catch up with the top sides like Manchester United because they're a class apart. I don't think that'll happen because my team of babies have only just learned to walk and you don't run before you learn to walk, so you don't. But in case I haven't mentioned it before now, we've got an awful lot of bad injuries, so we have. And we're all babies, so we are. Which means we've got no chance against Ipswich, so we haven't. Enjoy the game but don't expect too much. To be sure. No excuses,

David O'Leary

OWEN STICKS WITH BAYERN!

MATCH picked out Owen Hargreaves as one for the future ages ago, so when we were in Germany recently, we popped in to see how the Bayern Munich and England Under-21 midfielder was doing. We asked the Champions League-winning star, considered by some at Bayern to be the new Franz Beckenbauer, whether he fancied a move to England soon. "Bayern is the first club I've ever been at, so I don't really know," he shrugged. "I moved over here when I was 16 years old and before that in Canada I was just messing about, playing once or twice a week. Bayern is the first club I've ever really seen. The organisation is terrific, we have a great squad and we always play in the big tournaments, so it's perfect. Things have been going well since I was 16. I made the jump to Bayern, then I moved up a couple of teams after playing in the youths and the reserves. I'm happy that everything keeps taking a higher step." Hmm. He sounds happy. We're just worried that he's getting too used to those lederhosen!

THIERRY'S INJURY TERROR!

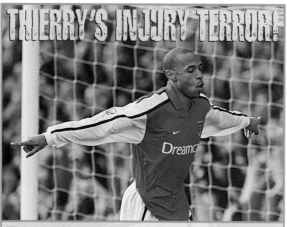

Thierry Henry might make playing football look easy, but the France striker says holding down a place in the first team can be a worrying business. At a top club like Arsenal, there are always quality strikers trying to pinch your place in the starting line-up, and as he explained to Route 1, any injury is a scary one! **"When you suffer an injury you're worried about getting better, but you're also a bit worried about someone taking your place in the side,"** said Henry. **"Okay, we're all together and in the team, but you feel so much better when you're actually out on the pitch. That's why sometimes when you're saying, 'Oh we play too many games', it's still always better to be on the pitch than off it. It can be the most difficult thing when you have a bad injury."** We don't know what Thierry's worried about. The ace marksman should never have any problems getting a game.

SPOT THE LEG!

There's £5 for anyone who can find the missing leg of Dutch defender Frank de Boer!

SLEEPING BECKS!

David Beckham is regularly described as 'a dreamboat' by lovesick ladies. And now it seems an appropriate nickname for the Manchester United star after Route 1 discovered the amount of time Dave spends dreaming about football. **"I've woken up so many times to find I've just re-lived a free-kick into the top corner or played in a big international,"** revealed Becks. **"I suppose it shows that football is a huge part of my life. It was everything until my family came along. Now they're my main priority, but football is still massively important to me. Recently, I've had dreams about winning a trophy with England, showing it to the fans and being as proud as anything. It felt good in my dreams, so it would be something else if I could do it in real life."** Now you really are dreaming Becks!

RYAN GIGGS
Manchester United

Steve Harper celebrates a win for the Toon Army.

Paul Gascoigne started out as a Newcastle trainee in 1985.

Barry Venison lifts the 1993 Division One championship.

Warren Barton reminds himself who he plays for!

Newcastle old boys Steve Watson, Darren Peacock and David Batty.

THE TOON!

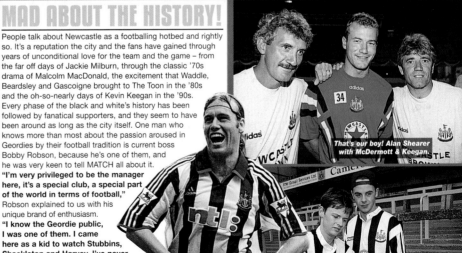

MATCH investigates why the Toon Army are so passionate about **Newcastle United**!

THEY SAY NEWCASTLE FANS BLEED BLACK AND white – and if you've ever stepped foot inside St James' Park on a matchday, you certainly won't doubt it! Jam-packed with passionate Geordies, it's hard to imagine that the 52,000 supporters have a life outside the stadium as they live and breathe Newcastle United.

Players who have shown the same pride and affection for the Toon Army are rewarded with god-like status. Today's captain Alan Shearer has joined the likes of Jackie Milburn, Malcolm MacDonald, Kevin Keegan, Paul Gascoigne, Andy Cole and Peter Beardsley in the hall of fame.

With such a long and varied history, and with the ground in a prime city centre location, the team has always played an important role in the lives of the local community. There are no fans more jubilant when glory comes their way, such as the league titles at the turn of the 1900s, the triple FA Cup success in the '50s and European triumph in the '60s. And supporters have never been more gutted when glory has been snatched from the Toon Army's grasp – like in the recent successive FA Cup final defeats at Wembley.

The current crop of Newcastle players – plus genial boss Bobby Robson – tell MATCH all about the famous Geordie spirit, the history of the club, the ace new stadium and the key figures around St James' Park. Now you can find out why the Magpies fans are so mad about the Toon!

Kevin Keegan was a hero on Tyneside from 1982-83.

Peter Beardsley leads the side out in the 1996 Charity Shield.

That's our boy! Alan Shearer with McDermott & Keegan.

Celebrity Newcastle fans Ant and Dec!

MAD ABOUT THE HISTORY!

People talk about Newcastle as a footballing hotbed and rightly so. It's a reputation the city and the fans have gained through years of unconditional love for the team and the game – from the far off days of Jackie Milburn, through the classic '70s drama of Malcolm MacDonald, the excitement that Waddle, Beardsley and Gascoigne brought to The Toon in the '80s and the oh-so-nearly days of Kevin Keegan in the '90s. Every phase of the black and white's history has been followed by fanatical supporters, and they seem to have been around as long as the city itself. One man who knows more than most about the passion aroused in Geordies by their football tradition is current boss Bobby Robson, because he's one of them, and he was very keen to tell MATCH all about it.

"I'm very privileged to be the manager here, it's a special club, a special part of the world in terms of football," Robson explained to us with his unique brand of enthusiasm.

"I know the Geordie public, I was one of them. I came here as a kid to watch Stubbins, Shackleton and Harvey. I've never lost that love and devotion for the club. Even when I was the manager of England, I always looked for Newcastle's result. I've often wondered why I never signed for the club as a player when I was 17 years old. I would have loved to play for Newcastle United – I really would have loved that."

Peter Beardsley
1983-1987 & 1993-1997

Lee Clark
1989-1997

Steve Howey
1989-2000

Robbie Elliott
1991-1997

Steve Watson
1991-1998

MAD ABOUT THE GEORDIE SPIRIT!

The people of Newcastle love to see local lads doing well for the club and there have been plenty of those over the years – see the pictures above! The fans also want local people to run the club because they know what being in the Toon Army means. Alan Shearer has become a legend at his local club. **"The black and white is drummed into you and that's how I became a fan. I always wanted to play for the club, as I'm sure most boys in Newcastle want to today. It's part and parcel of growing up in the city that your mums – and particularly your dads – want you to watch and play for Newcastle,"** says Shearer. **"Having a Geordie chairman as well means the fans feel they can relate to us. They all want to know what's going on at the club and it's very important to continue that tradition."**

But it's not just Shearer who feels a special bond with the fans. Young striker Shola Ameobi, who is cheered on by friends in the crowd, enjoys the same feeling. **"As a Newcastle fan I looked up to players in the past and now I'm playing I know what it must have been like for them. The crowd like to see a local lad playing well, so that's helped me along too. Hearing the crowd gives me confidence and the reception I've had ever since I've come into the team has been fantastic."**

MAD ABOUT THE FANS!

Newcastle were in big trouble back in 1992. With the season reaching its climax, the prospect of a terrifying drop into the old Division Three loomed for The Magpies and things looked ominous. But amazingly, St James' Park was still jam-packed for every home fixture. Why? Because Newcastle fans provide unfailing support for their team through thick and thin. The Toon Army – as the fans are collectively called – is like a 12th man to the team and everyone who's played for the club is always quick to sing their praises. **"Newcastle fans are just the best supporters in the world,"** admitted superstar midfielder Kieron Dyer. **"They're second to none. They treat football like a religion. Everything that happens in Newcastle is to do with football. I've heard that the newspapers can sell just because of Newcastle being on the back pages. Honestly, they really are amazing! It's like we always have a goal head start and the support of the fans is probably the reason why I've settled in so well at the club – they've taken me in and made my life very easy."**

The famous Toon Army supporting their boys.

MAD ABOUT THE MANAGER!

When Kevin Keegan handed in his surprise resignation in March 1997, Newcastle tried to sign the one man they thought could bring success back to the club – Bobby Robson. But the ex-England boss was under contract with Barcelona and the club had to wait two and a half years to get their man, with Kenny Dalglish and Ruud Gullit both failing to meet the demands of the Toon Army. He inherited a team struggling against relegation just two months into the 1999-2000 season. **"I don't think anybody realised – until they'd met him and he'd had his first little talk – how important Bobby was to this club,"** said Warren Barton, who witnessed Robson's first team-talk. **"We were in a dire position and without him the club would have gone down – at the age of 75 that's fantastic! Bobby coming here was massive."**

Robson has long been recognised as a great football coach and he's worked well with both youngsters and seniors to pass on his knowledge and improve their game. Young striker Carl Cort is one of his grateful recipients. **"It's fantastic to be able to play under a manager like Bobby Robson,"** Cort told us. **"No-one has the experience and knowledge that he does. I knew as soon as I came here that it'd be beneficial for my career at club and international level. I didn't think there was anywhere better to come to further my career."**

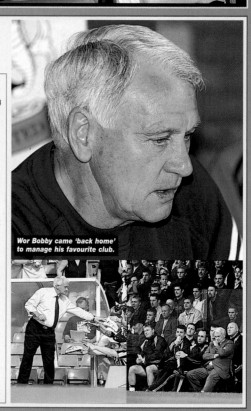
Wor Bobby came 'back home' to manage his favourite club.

MAD ABOUT LOCAL RIVALRY!

Newcastle fans don't like their Sunderland rivals at the best of times – let alone when the two sides meet for the passionate North East derby. The players soon learn how much it means to the Toon Army, as defender Warren Barton – a veteran of many North East derbies – revealed. **"Football rivalry used to be about Liverpool and Everton in Merseyside and Arsenal versus Tottenham in London. But now it's all about the North East, which is great because the people up here are fanatics, there's no question about that. They all want to see football played the right way as well because they love the game."**

Newcastle have a bitter rivalry with Sunderland.

Warren Barton and Steve Harper helping out local Newcastle lads.

Barton says the youngsters need to 'weight' for a first-team place!

Brian Kerr with Gary and Stephen Caldwell.

Young hopefuls Michael Chopra and Bradley Orr.

MAD ABOUT THE YOUTH SET-UP!

After years in the wilderness, the Newcastle academy is coming up trumps as players like Aaron Hughes and Shola Ameobi have made the breakthrough from the youth set-up to the club's first team. With a great academy system in place and some excellent facilities, the club has no problems in attracting young players, as defender Aaron Hughes told us: **"The football, the people and the coaching staff attracted me to Newcastle. They're really friendly and warm here, like the people in Northern Ireland – they really looked after me when I first came over."**

Hughes worked his way up from being a young apprentice to a regular reserve team player before making his debut in a UEFA Cup tie against Barcelona! And the Irishman has received help from the club at every stage of his development. **"The players have always helped me. I don't think there's ever been any pressure on me, I'm just expected to do my best and be happy with the way I play. If I do my best and still don't end up being in the first team regularly, then fair enough."**

But Hughes has been able to cut it as a first-team regular and he was joined last season by the promising Shola Ameobi, who stepped in for the injured £7 million striker Carl Cort. **"The club has done really well with its youth players and a few of them are coming through,"** Ameobi explained. **"It's tremendous and the boss has been great with the young players. He's never doubted us when he's brought us into the first team."**

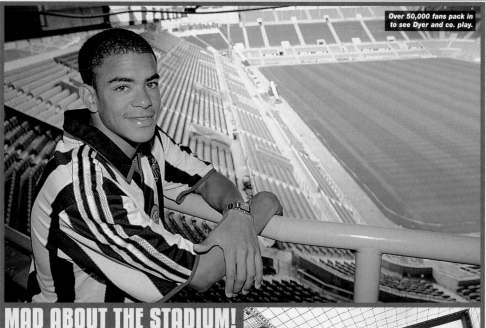

Over 50,000 fans pack in to see Dyer and co. play.

The atmosphere is intimidating for visiting players and fans.

MAD ABOUT THE STADIUM!

Even before the latest redevelopment work, St James' Park was one of the most intimidating stadiums in the country – but it's even more scary now the capacity has been raised by almost 20,000 to 52,219. **"The atmosphere's absolutely brilliant at St James Park,"** Rob Lee told us. **"It was always good but with the extra stand, the whole atmosphere of the place is even more impressive now. When you've got around 52,000 screaming Geordies behind you, that's all the motivation you need. It's quite daunting for the opposition fans now, so it's more important to do well when we're at home."**

The stadium is on raised ground near Newcastle city centre and it's filled to the brim with season ticket holders on every single matchday. The fans are proud of their historic stadium as Alan Shearer – who stood on the terraces himself – knows well. **"The stadium is second to none, it's unbelievable,"** said the Magpies skipper. **"It's what the people of Newcastle deserve. The supporters are very proud of it and we know we can fill it every week because of the way the fans are."**

Geordies worship Alan Shearer like he's a god!

NEWCASTLE 9 BROWN ALE

HOWAY THE LADS !

MAD ABOUT ALAN SHEARER!

Alan Shearer is a god on Tyneside, it's as simple as that. The hero worship began on the day the striker was unveiled as the club's £15 million record signing in July 1996, when thousands of supporters turned up at St James' Park to welcome the striker home to his native North East. But it's not just the fans who worship him – staff see him as an integral part of the club and the players respect his ability and stature too, as 'keeper Shay Given told us. **"He's one of the best forwards in the world and that's evident whether he's playing in a game or training,"** said Given. **"But it's great for me to face him every day in training. It improves my game and prepares me well for when I have to face top-class opposition."**

FOOTY MAD!

There's always room for a laugh at someone else's expense – as this selection of classic **MATCH** action pics shows.

THEY SAID WHAT!

MATCH looks back at some of the gems we overheard during last season…

"When I was younger, I told my mum and dad I didn't enjoy football and that I never wanted to play it again." Leeds manager David O'Leary would be pleased that his star striker Alan Smith quickly changed his mind.

"It was a little bit of a ding dong without much music, really. But we've ground out a result." Bobby Robson gets a little confused after his Newcastle side worked hard to pull off a valuable Premiership victory.

"A foreigner or an Englishman, it doesn't matter. I already feel sorry for him." Ruud 'I'm not bitter' Gullit welcomes Swedish-born Sven Goran Eriksson to the unenviable task that is the England manager's job.

"I don't think King should really be concerning himself with slagging off proven Premiership goalscorers. He has neither the track record as a manager nor standing in the game, to pass such unwarranted comments on me." Stan Collymore's reply to Swindon manager Andy King, who threatened to resign if the club signed Collymore behind his back.

"He should sign a new long-term contract with United, persuade his missus to have a few more bairns and then get as much rest as he can." The worldly-wise Brian Clough offers some advice to Old Trafford star David Beckham.

"I don't think Darius is as elegant as Dwight. He's also quieter – and he's in his own bed by 11pm at night!" Aston Villa boss John Gregory responds to claims that Darius Vassell is similar to ex-Villan Dwight Yorke.

"I don't like the north. It's always raining, it's very cold and I don't like all those little houses." West Ham striker Frederic Kanoute wastes no time in ruling himself out of a move to Manchester United.

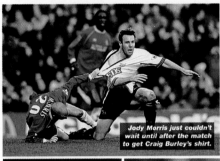

Jody Morris just couldn't wait until after the match to get Craig Burley's shirt.

Emile forgets the golden rule – you should always check for toilet roll first.

The 'standing on one leg' competition was getting ridiculous.

Big Stuart thought no-one was looking and got all poncey.

The referee knew exactly who'd nicked his hairspray.

Was the Man. City job too massive for Joe Royle or was it vice versa?

Real Madrid fans are told when the team scores, as if the ball going in the net isn't clear enough!

"That was a close one Stevie, you nearly smiled there mate."

Henry tries to steal the flag…

…but Dave Bassett is quick to grass him up.

Surely tackled from a behind, thinks a shocked Gary Neville…

…while Rufus Brevett rethinks his tactics!

Michael Mols, just before he sacked his fashion consultant.

Topless footy is all the rage at Dagenham & Redbridge.

"You can clean me car next, pal."

Who's the dummy?

I wish he'd clean his teeth before these games!

Even with your eyes shut, Palace v Wimbledon was a painful experience.

Robbie Keane is asked if Leeds can win the league.

The Old Trafford ballet lessons were paying off.

The years of close nose control practise started to pay off at Everton…

…while the static on the ball caused a freak reaction to Karembeu's hair!

40 M

ROBERT PIRES
Arsenal

MATCH
ENTERTAINERS

2002
FIFA WORLD CUP
KOREA JAPAN
© 1999 FIFA TM

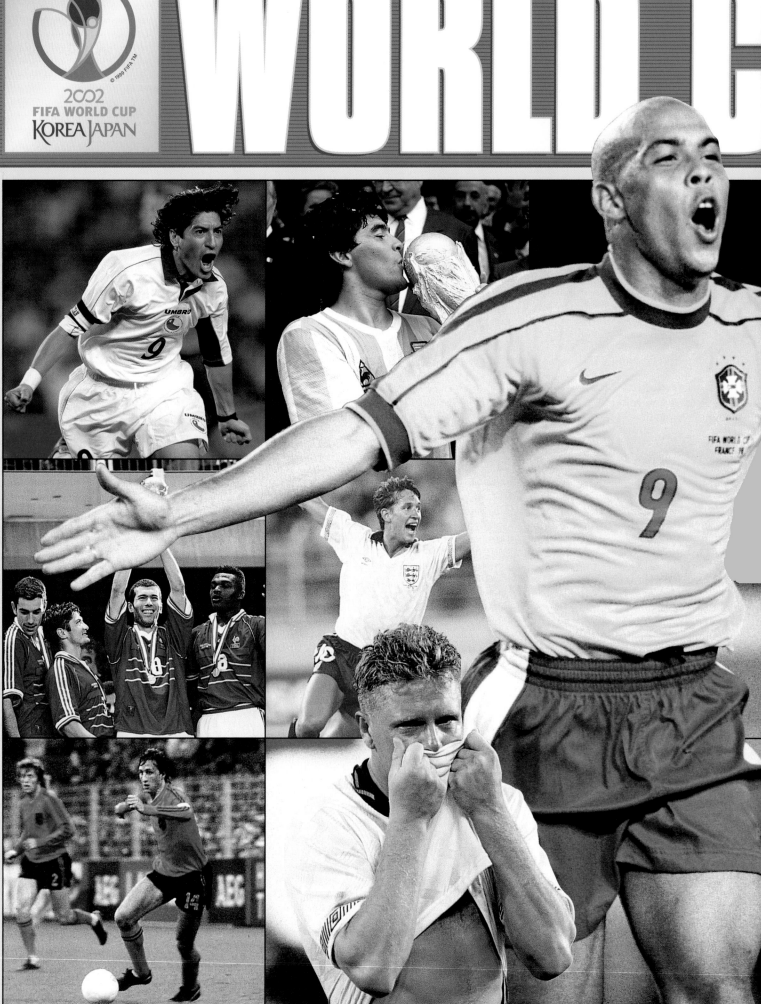

UP 2002

MATCH can't wait till the 2002 World Cup kicks off! Here's our guide to what you can expect.

REMEMBER THE 2001 SUMMER? IT WAS PRETTY boring wasn't it? No major championships were held to keep us occupied and we all had to put up with playing footy down the park ourselves. But it'll be different in June 2002, because the World Cup will be here again… we can't wait!

France '98 was such a great tournament – a festival of goals, action, comebacks and top players fighting it out for the ultimate trophy in football. It would have been more enjoyable if England had beaten Argentina and made it to the quarter-finals – but who could forget that screaming Beckham free-kick which thundered into the Colombia net or the spectacular solo effort from Michael Owen against Batistuta's Argentina? Thankfully, the entertainment didn't stop once England had gone home, with Croatia making it to the semi-finals after hammering Germany 3-0 and Dennis Bergkamp's winning volley against Argentina in the quarters. Now you can get ready to experience it all again!

In 2002, for the first time, the World Cup will be hosted by two nations – Japan and South Korea. Half of the tickets have gone to fanatical supporters in those countries who can't wait to see the world's finest in their own homelands.

We couldn't wait to find out everything about the football-mad host countries and meet the official mascots! So read on to see what MATCH discovered and get ready to fill-in the progress of the teams in the handy World Cup chart.

WORLD CUP FACTFILE

First Game: May 31, 2002 in Seoul, South Korea
Final: June 30, 2002 in Yokohama Stadium, Japan
South Korean Host Cities: Seoul, Suwon, Daejeon, Daegu, Ulsan, Busan, Gwangju, Seogwipo, Jeonju, Incheon
Japanese Host Cities: Yokohama, Sapporo, Miyagi, Niigata, Ibaraki, Saitama, Shizuoka, Osaka, Kobe, Oita
Automatic Qualifiers: Japan, South Korea & France

ASIA

SOUTH KOREA

JAPAN

SEOUL

SOUTH KOREA FACTFILE

Association: South Korea Football Association
Joined FIFA: 1948
Honours: Asian Cup 1956, 1960; Asian Cup runners-up 1972, 1980, 1988; Asian Games 1978, 1986
Players: 736,000
Website: www.kfa.or.kr
Coach: Gus Hiddink
Hiddink was appointed in Nov. 2000 and his contract runs until June 30. South Korea hope he will have just as much success in this World Cup as the last, where he led Holland to the semi-finals.
Capital: Seoul
Population: 46.9 million
Leader: President Kim Dae-jung
Main industries: Shipbuilding & consumer electronics

INFO ON SOUTH KOREA

★ Historians believe that football was introduced to the area around 1880 by British marines. There are, however, no records of football being played until the country was annexed by Japan in 1910.

★ The South Korean FA was closed down in 1938 when Japan ruled the country as a colony, and from 1936 the best Korean players were even allowed to play for the Japanese national side – until the country was liberated in 1945.

★ Out of all the Asian countries, South Korea holds the record for qualifying for the most World Cup Finals. Neighbouring North Korea is the most successful Asian nation to date though – having reached the quarter-final stages in 1966.

WORLD CUP RECORD

✚ SWITZERLAND ★ 1954		
	0 v 9	HUNGARY
	0 v 7	TURKEY
MEXICO ★ 1986		
	1 v 3	ARGENTINA
	1 v 1	BULGARIA
	2 v 3	ITALY
ITALY ★ 1990		
	0 v 2	BELGIUM
	1 v 3	SPAIN
	0 v 1	URUGUAY
USA ★ 1994		
	2 v 2	SPAIN
	0 v 0	BOLIVIA
	2 v 3	GERMANY
FRANCE ★ 1998		
	1 v 3	MEXICO
	0 v 5	HOLLAND
	1 v 1	BELGIUM

MATCH SOUTH KOREAN & JAPANESE FOOTBALL STADIUMS

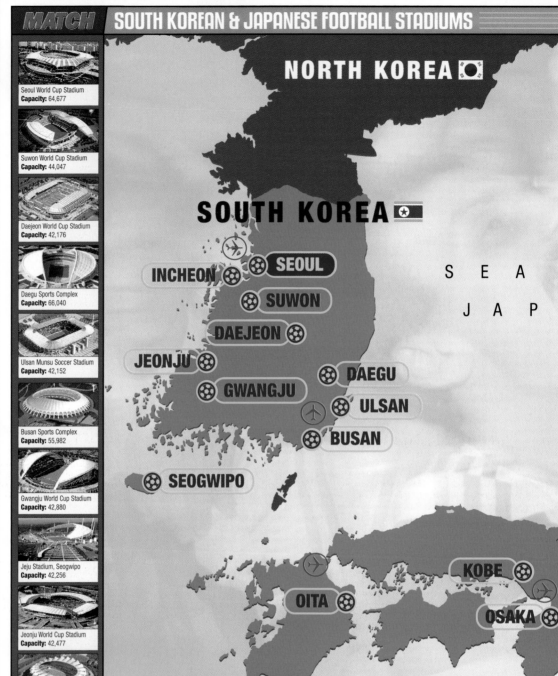

NORTH KOREA

SOUTH KOREA

SEA OF JAPAN

INCHEON
SEOUL
SUWON
DAEJEON
JEONJU
GWANGJU
DAEGU
ULSAN
BUSAN
SEOGWIPO

KOBE
OITA
OSAKA

Seoul World Cup Stadium
Capacity: 64,677

Suwon World Cup Stadium
Capacity: 44,047

Daejeon World Cup Stadium
Capacity: 42,176

Daegu Sports Complex
Capacity: 66,040

Ulsan Munsu Soccer Stadium
Capacity: 42,152

Busan Sports Complex
Capacity: 55,982

Gwangju World Cup Stadium
Capacity: 42,880

Jeju Stadium, Seogwipo
Capacity: 42,256

Jeonju World Cup Stadium
Capacity: 42,477

Incheon Munhak Stadium
Capacity: 52,630

MEET THE MASCOTS!

The mascots are based on energy particles in the air.

THE MASCOTS FOR THE 2002 WORLD Cup have now been revealed. Fittingly, for a new century and for two countries at the forefront of technology, the tournament's mascots are all 3D computer-animated cartoon characters, replacing the dated-looking, hand-drawn creatures of past tournaments. The mascots are collectively known as 'spherics' and they symbolise energy particles in the air. Got that? Good! The drawings of the mascots were first introduced to the public two years ago, but it wasn't until May 2000 that their names were decided. Over 10,000 young fans across Japan and South Korea were invited to vote for the names in chains of McDonald's restaurants, the official World Cup sponsors. They voted for 'Ato' as the name of the team coach (that's the taller one in the picture!), and 'Nik' and 'Kaz' as the names of the two players.

ASIA

SAPPORO

MIYAGI

NIIGATA

JAPAN

SAITAMA

TOKYO

IBARAKI

YOKOHAMA

SHIZUOKA

P A C I F I C
O C E A N

| 0 | | 200 | | 400 kms |

| 0 | 100 | | 200 miles | |

International Stadium
Capacity: 70,564

Sapporo Dome Stadium
Capacity: 42,122

Miyagi Stadium
Capacity: 49,133

Niigata Stadium
Capacity: 42,700

Ibaraki Soccer Stadium
Capacity: 41,800

Saitama Stadium
Capacity: 63,700

Shizuoka Stadium Ecopa
Capacity: 51,349

Nagai Stadium, Osaka
Capacity: 50,000

Kobe Wing Stadium
Capacity: 42,000

Oita Stadium Big Eye
Capacity: 43,000

TOKYO

JAPAN FACTFILE

Association: Football Association of Japan

Joined FIFA: 1929

Honours: 1968 Olympics bronze medal & 1992 Asian Cup

Players: 796,873

Website: www.jfa.or.jp

Coach: Philippe Troussier
The Frenchman managed South Africa at the 1998 World Cup, where they drew with Denmark and Saudi Arabia but lost to France. Troussier was chosen to coach the Japanese national side after this. His contract with Japan runs out at the end of June 2002, after the World Cup Finals end.

Capital: Tokyo

Population: 126.5 million

Leader: Yoshiro Mori

Main industries: Construction & industry

INFO ON JAPAN

★ Football is believed to have been brought to Japanese shores by an Englishman – Lieutenant Commander Douglas of the Royal Navy – in 1873. He was a teacher at the naval academy in Tokyo and taught football in his spare time.

★ The first ever game in Japan's professional league, the J-League, kicked off on May 15, 1993 when a full house of 59,626 fans saw Verdy Kawasaki play Yokohama Marinos. The league became an overnight sensation and has drawn big crowds ever since.

★ Two years ago, the Japanese Football Association brought in a player contract system which groups players into three different wage categories – A, B and C with A being the highest. To qualify for an 'A' contract, players must play a certain amount of time in league and cup matches or have been a 'C' category player for three years.

★ You won't find normal football fare on sale at Japan's national football stadium in Tokyo. Rather than snacking on a meat pie or hamburger, you can treat yourself to some fried noodles or octopus dumplings instead. You first then!

★ Japan became the first ever Asian side to play at Wembley when they took on England in a friendly tournament, the Umbro International Trophy, in June 1995. Japan lost 2-1, with Ihara scoring for Japan and Anderton and Platt on the scoresheet for England.

WORLD CUP RECORD

FRANCE ★ 1998

●	0 v 1	FRANCE
●	0 v 1	ARGENTINA
●	0 v 1	CROATIA
●	1 v 2	JAMAICA

TICKET TROUBLE!

FANS TRAVELLING TO WATCH THE WORLD
Cup will not only pay the earth to travel to Asia, they'll also be forking out a lot of cash for tickets. The average price to watch a match at France '98 was £37, but that rockets to £97 in Japan or South Korea. Fans can get a £40 ticket for a group game, but they'll be stuck behind the goals – a good view will set supporters back £100! If you think that's too much, you certainly won't have applied for a prime view seat for the final – priced at a massive £500! FIFA justified these prices by saying it costs a lot to stage matches in Japan and South Korea.

Many tickets sold out early to fans from the two host nations.

FANATICAL FAR EAST!

THIS WILL BE THE FIRST TIME THAT THE
World Cup has been held on the continent of Asia and the football-mad fans over there can hardly wait! There is a big following for English football in the Far East, but Japan has its own division, the J-League, which attracts some big crowds. Hooliganism is hardly heard of in Japan and South Korea, and Japanese fans even stay behind after J-League matches to clear up litter!

To illustrate just how fanatical the Japanese are about football, you just have to look at their best-known player – Hidetoshi Nakata – who shot to fame when he starred for Japan at the 1998 World Cup in France. After the tournament, Nakata joined Italian outfit Perugia and the club sold more than 70,000 'Nakata 7' shirts in Japan during his one season at the club. The midfielder, who now plays for top side Roma, gets 200,000 hits a day on his official website and among the products that he endorses are designer names Prada, Armani… and a Japanese supermarket!

Nakata is a commercial dream for Italian clubs.

HOW TO USE YOUR FILL-IN CHART!

BY THE TIME CHRISTMAS DAY comes around, the draw will have been made for the World Cup and we'll know which teams will travel to compete in these Finals. So get your pen out and start scribbling because you can already fill in the first part of your chart. Just read the instructions below, but you will need a copy of the full draw for Japan/South Korea 2002 – this will be printed in MATCH.

GROUP STAGES

THERE ARE EIGHT GROUPS WHICH include all 32 teams, from Groups A to H. Each of these groups contain four teams which have been seeded. France, as 1998 World Cup winners, are seeded as A1, while teams that qualified via a play-off are seeded fourth – eg A4 or B4. Write the teams down in the group in which they've been drawn AND in their seeding order – a top side drawn in Group B will be B1. The rest will be draw in seeding order, from B2 down to B4!

SECOND ROUND

AS THE FINALS GET UNDERWAY you'll be able to fill-in your chart further. For example, in the second round the Winners of Group A will play the Runners-up in Group F. Just follow the instructions in the second round boxes, as shown below.

QUARTER-FINALS

EACH SECOND ROUND MATCH has a game number. For example, the match involving the Group A Winners versus the Group F Runners-Up is called Game 5. This'll help you fill in the quarter-finals box, eg the Game 5 Winners versus the Game 7 Winners.

SEMI-FINALS

EACH QUARTER-FINAL (QF) IS labelled from A to D. The winners go into the semi-final boxes, eg the QF C Winners play the QF D Winners.

FINAL & PLAY-OFF

The winners from the semi-finals (SF) go into the final while both the losers go into the third-place play-off. Fill in your chart once the games have been played and fill in the scores to keep a record of what actually happened!

FILL-IN CHART

2002 WORLD CUP SOUTH KOREA AND JAPAN

MATCH

★ SOUTH KOREA

★ GROUP A ★

A1	France
A2	
A3	
A4	

FIXTURES: France v A2, 8:30pm **May 31** in **Seoul**; A3 v A4, 6:00pm **Jun 1** in **Ulsan**; France v A3, 3:30pm **Jun 6** in **Busan**; A2 v A4, 8:30pm **Jun 6** in **Daegu**; A2 v A3, 3:30pm **Jun 11** in **Suwon**; France v A4, 3:30pm **Jun 11** in **Incheon**

★ GROUP B ★

B1	
B2	
B3	
B4	

FIXTURES: B3 v B4, 4:30pm **Jun 2** in **Busan**; B1 v B2, 8:30pm **Jun 2** in **Gwangju**; B2 v B4, 3:30pm **Jun 8** in **Daegu**; B1 v B3, 6:00pm **Jun 7** in **Jeonju**; B2 v B3 8:30pm **Jun 12** in **Seogwipo**; B1 v B4, 8:30pm **Jun 12** in **Daejeon**

★ GROUP C ★

C1	
C2	
C3	
C4	

FIXTURES: C1 v C2, 6:00pm **Jun 3** in **Ulsan**; C3 v C4, 3:30pm **Jun 4** in **Gwangju**; C1 v C3, 8:30pm **Jun 8** in **Seogwipo**; C4 v C2, 6:00pm **Jun 9** in **Incheon**; C4 v C1, 3:30pm **Jun 13** in **Suwon**; C2 v C3, 8:30pm **Jun 13** in **Seoul**

★ GROUP D ★

D1	South Korea
D2	
D3	
D4	

FIXTURES: S. Korea v D2, 8:30pm **Jun 4** in **Busan**; D3 v D4, 6:00pm **Jun 5** in **Suwon**; S. Korea v D3, 3:30pm **Jun 10** in **Daegu**; D2 v D4, 8:30pm **Jun 10** in **Jeonju**; D2 v D3, 8:30pm **Jun 14** in **Daejeon**; S. Korea v D4, 8:30pm **Jun 14** in **Incheon**

★ JAPAN ★

★ GROUP E ★

E1	
E2	
E3	
E4	

FIXTURES: E1 v E2, 8:30pm **Jun 1** in **Sapporo**; E3 v E4, 3:30pm **Jun 1** in **Niigata**; E1 v E3, 8:30pm **Jun 5** in **Ibaraki**; E4 v E2, 6:00pm **Jun 6** in **Saitama**; E2 v E3, 8:30pm **Jun 11** in **Yokohama**; E1 v E4, 8:30pm **Jun 11** in **Shizuoka**

★ GROUP F ★

F1	
F2	
F3	
F4	

FIXTURES: F1 v F2, 6:30pm **Jun 2** in **Ibaraki**; F3 v F4, 2:30pm **Jun 2** in **Saitama**; F1 v F3, 8:30pm **Jun 7** in **Sapporo**; F2 v F4, 3:30pm **Jun 7** in **Kobe**; F2 v F3, 3:30pm **Jun 12** in **Osaka**; F1 v F4, 3:30pm **June 12** in **Miyagi**

★ GROUP G ★

G1	
G2	
G3	
G4	

FIXTURES: G1 v G2, 8:30pm **Jun 3** in **Sapporo**; G3 v G4, 3:30pm **Jun 3** in **Niigata**; G1 v G3, 6:00pm **Jun 8** in **Ibaraki**; G2 v G4, 3:30pm **Jun 9** in **Miyagi**; G2 v G3, 8:30pm **Jun 13** in **Yokohama**; G4 v G1, 8:30pm **Jun 13** in **Oita**

★ GROUP H ★

H1	Japan
H2	
H3	
H4	

FIXTURES: Japan v H2, 6:00pm **Jun 4** in **Saitama**; H3 v H4, 3:30pm **Jun 5** in **Kobe**; Japan v H3 **Jun 9** in **Yokohama**; H4 v H2, 6:00pm **Jun 10** in **Oita**; H2 v H3, 3:30pm **Jun 14** in **Shizuoka**; H4 v Japan, 3:30pm **Jun 14** in **Osaka**

SECOND ROUND ★ GAME 1

| Group E Winners | |
| Group B Runners-up | |

DATE: June 15 **TIME:** 3:30pm **VENUE:** Seogwipo

SECOND ROUND ★ GAME 2

| Group B Winners | |
| Group E Runners-up | |

DATE: June 16 **TIME:** 8:30pm **VENUE:** Suwon

SECOND ROUND ★ GAME 3

| Group G Winners | |
| Group D Runners-up | |

DATE: June 17 **TIME:** 3:30pm **VENUE:** Jeonju

SECOND ROUND ★ GAME 4

| Group D Winners | |
| Group G Runners-up | |

DATE: June 18 **TIME:** 8:30pm **VENUE:** Daejeon

SECOND ROUND ★ GAME 5

| Group A Winners | |
| Group F Runners-up | |

DATE: June 15 **TIME:** 8:30pm **VENUE:** Niigata

SECOND ROUND ★ GAME 6

| Group F Winners | |
| Group A Runners-up | |

DATE: June 16 **TIME:** 3:30pm **VENUE:** Oita

SECOND ROUND ★ GAME 7

| Group C Winners | |
| Group H Runners-up | |

DATE: June 17 **TIME:** 8:30pm **VENUE:** Kobe

SECOND ROUND ★ GAME 8

| Group H Winners | |
| Group C Runners-up | |

DATE: June 18 **TIME:** 3:30pm **VENUE:** Miyagi

QUARTER-FINAL ★ A

Game 1 Winners	
Game 3 Winners	

DATE: June 21 **TIME:** 8:30pm **VENUE:** Ulsan

SEMI-FINAL ★ ONE

QF A Winners	
QF B Winners	

DATE: June 25 **TIME:** 8:30pm **VENUE:** Seoul

QUARTER-FINAL ★ B

Game 2 Winners	
Game 4 Winners	

DATE: June 22 **TIME:** 3:30pm **VENUE:** Gwangju

2002 FIFA WORLD CUP KOREA JAPAN

THIRD PLACE PLAY-OFF ★

SF ONE Runners-up	
SF TWO Runners-up	

DATE: June 29 **TIME:** 8:00pm **VENUE:** Daegu

★ THE FINAL ★

SF ONE Winners	
SF TWO Winners	

DATE: June 30 **TIME:** 8:00pm **VENUE:** Yokohama

QUARTER-FINAL ★ C

Game 5 Winners	
Game 7 Winners	

DATE: June 21 **TIME:** 3:30pm **VENUE:** Shizuoka

SEMI-FINAL ★ TWO

QF C Winners	
QF D Winners	

DATE: June 26 **TIME:** 8:30pm **VENUE:** Saitama

QUARTER-FINAL ★ D

Game 6 Winners	
Game 8 Winners	

DATE: June 22 **TIME:** 8:30pm **VENUE:** Osaka

THE FINAL WHISTLE

HOW DID YOU SCORE?
See how you get on with these footy teasers, remember there's a point for each correct answer which can be checked on pages 106 & 107.

CROSSWORD

Use your footy knowledge to solve the crossword below!

Second XI

The most successful team of the last decade has to be Man. United. But how much do you know about them?

1 How many times have Manchester United won the Premiership title?

2 Which player broke the United transfer record when he signed in August 1998 for £12.6 million?

3 Roy Keane is inspirational for the Old Trafford outfit, but can you remember the captain's two previous clubs?

4 Against which Second Division club did a young David Beckham make his first-team debut as a sub in the League Cup way back in September 1992?

5 'Captain Marvel' Bryan Robson left United in 1994. How many years had he been at Old Trafford and which club did he move to?

6 Legend Eric Cantona often caused controversy, but which side was the star playing against when he committed his infamous kung-fu kick on a fan?

7 Beckham scored his wonder goal on the first day of the season in August 1996, chipping the 'keeper from 57 yards. But who was between the posts and which team was he playing for?

8 Manchester United won the FA Cup in 1999 en route to the treble, beating Newcastle 2-0. Can you name their two goalscorers?

9 Which top Italian side did Alex Ferguson's charges beat in the 1999 Champions League semi-finals and what was the aggregate score over the two legs?

10 True or false? Roy Keane did not play in the 1999 European Cup Final against Bayern Munich.

11 The Red Devils will lose Sir Alex Ferguson as manager in May 2002 when he retires. Exactly how many seasons will he have been manager of the club?

Celebration time again for the Man. United lads.

ACROSS
1. City which hosted the 2001 FA Cup final (7)
4. Leicester and Scotland centre-back, Matt (7)
9. Michael, young Liverpool and England striker (4)
10. Country for which Stan Collymore departed Bradford (5)
11. Nickname associated with a Barnsley man (4)
12. Hull City's club emblem (5)
16. Olivier, French midfielder at Elland Road (7)
17. £18 million defender, Rio, of Leeds and England (9)
18. Manchester United's Welsh winger, Ryan (5)
20. David, manager of Nottingham Forest (5)
21. Norwegian striker, Ole Gunnar, at Old Trafford (9)
24. Mark, full-back of Aston Villa and Wales (7)
26. French midfielder, Emmanuel, sold by Arsenal to Barcelona (5)
30. Colin, ex-Swindon boss assisting Jim Smith at Derby (4)
31. The Wasps from Scotland's Recreation Park (5)
32. Newcastle and England star, Kieron (4)
33. Welsh Second Division club from the Vetch (7)
34. Michael, one-time Chelsea defender recruited by David O'Leary (7)

DOWN
1. Gary, former Blackburn full-back more recently at Ipswich (5)
2. Irish defender, Richard, transferred from Everton to Man. City (5)
3. Charlton's ex-Bolton South African, Mark (4)
4. Neil, Celtic's N. Ireland midfielder once at Filbert Street (6)
5. Italian club sharing the San Siro with AC Milan (5)
6. Club nickname of Aberdeen and Wimbledon (3,4)
7. German who scored the last goal at the old Wembley stadium (6)
13. Anfield's classy young England midfield man, Steven (7)
15. Stalwart N. Ireland centre-back, Gerry, with the Foxes (7)
16. Initials by which the Deepdale men are familiarly known (1,1,1)
19. Homeland of Everton's Joe-Max Moore (1,1,1)
20. Bristol Rovers' club nickname (5)
22. Glasgow Celtic's manager, Martin (6)
23. Robbie, all-action midfielder of Leicester and Wales (6)
25. Nicky, full-back in Birmingham's Worthington Cup campaign (5)
27. One-time Canary, Darren, now in the top flight (5)
28. Chelsea's England under-21 defender, John (5)
29. The Gunners' Nigerian forward, Nwankwo (4)

MATCH facts CODE BREAKER
CAN YOU SOLVE IT?

CRACK THE CODE!

| 13 | 14 | 23 | 23 | 18 | 2 |

| 6 | 18 | 2 | 14 |

THE PLAYER IS...

☐ ☐ ☐ ☐ ☐ I

☐ I ☐ ☐

WHO WON IT?
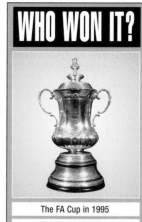
The FA Cup in 1995
1 POINT FOR CORRECT ANSWER

WHOSE NUMBER?
Which club shirt number is worn by these star players?

1 Ryan Giggs

2 Alan Shearer

3 Thierry Henry

4 Michael Owen

5 Lucas Radebe

1 POINT PER CORRECT ANSWER

THE GAFFERS!
How much do you know about the men in charge?

Name the manager of Southampton prior to January 2000?

How many trophies did Gianluca Vialli win as manger of Chelsea?

Graeme Souness has managed three English clubs. Name them.

True or False? George Graham used to play for Arsenal and Chelsea.

Which club did Harry Redknapp manage before his spell at West Ham?

1 POINT PER CORRECT ANSWER

connections...
Which Yorkshire club links Ron Atkinson with Howard Wilkinson?

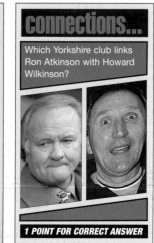

1 POINT FOR CORRECT ANSWER

STEVE McMANAMAN

Real Madrid

FOOTY REJE

Some footballers achieve their potential later in their careers.

THE 'FOOTY REJECTS' HEADLINE ISN'T meant to cause any offence – it's just a fact of life that hundreds of players are left heartbroken every year after being told they're not good enough to make the grade. Just look at the youngsters in your favourite club's youth or academy team. How many of them do you think will make it? Unfortunately, only two or three of them will make enough progress to graduate to the first team ranks.

Some players have no option but to fall away from the professional game and pursue their careers elsewhere. Others drop down a couple of levels, content to continue playing in the minor leagues. Then there are footy rejects who knuckle down, work hard to improve their game and keep faith in their own ability to find a different route to the top.

For every David Beckham, groomed for stardom since an early age and allowed to develop at one of the biggest clubs in the world, there's a footballer who's had to battle back from rejection to make it to the top. It's not just one or two players either – the Premiership's full of top stars who have been turned away early in their careers. And their stories should inspire all promising footballers out there to persevere and reach the top in the face of adversity.

Here, MATCH takes a look at some of the former 'footy rejects' who have achieved success the hard way.

AND HOW THEY BOUNCED BACK TO SUCCESS!

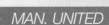

ANDY COLE ——————— MAN. UNITED

WHY WAS HE A REJECT? It never really worked out for Cole at his first club Arsenal, where he started out as an apprentice. His route to the first team was blocked by the likes of Alan Smith and Ian Wright so, after making a solitary league appearance, he moved to Bristol City for a fee of £500,000.

WHAT HAPPENED NEXT? Cole successfully relaunched his career with The Robins before being snapped up by Kevin Keegan, in charge of a resurgent Newcastle United. He became a lethal goalscorer with The Magpies, thriving up front with Peter Beardsley and winning the hearts of the Toon Army. After three seasons at St James' Park, the formidable striker made a shock move to Man. United in a £7 million deal and the rest, as they say, is history.

HAS HE PROVED THEM WRONG? Definitely, a thousand times over. Cole has been one of the best strikers in English football for several years and he's finally getting his chance on the international front following Sven Goran Eriksson's appointment as the new manager of the national side. Cole's goalscoring form has contributed to Man. United's domestic domination and he was instrumental in the 1999 treble triumph after forming a deadly partnership with close friend Dwight Yorke.

KEVIN PHILLIPS ——————— SUNDERLAND

WHY WAS HE A REJECT? Kevin was a YTS lad on the books of Southampton when he was told, a year into his stay, that he wasn't going to cut it as a striker but had a chance if he switched to right-back. He changed positions, but was released a year later.

WHAT HAPPENED NEXT? Undeterred, Kev went back home to Hertfordshire and earned some cash as a warehouse boy in a bread factory before landing a trial with local side Baldock Town. He starred in attack for the non-leaguers before being snapped up by Watford and did enough with The Hornets to attract interest from Sunderland, who signed him in the summer of 1997 for £325,000.

HAS HE PROVED THEM WRONG?
Absolutely! Phillips has been an incredible hit at Sunderland, scoring 29 goals in 43 league games in his first season, then 23 in 26 as the Black Cats won promotion to the Premiership. In 1999-2000, his first top-flight campaign, he scored 30 league goals to win the English and European Golden Boot award; he also finished runner-up in the 2000 PFA Player Of The Year awards. His goalscoring won him a place in England's Euro 2000 squad, but he didn't get a chance to play. Nevertheless, Southampton will be seething that they let the striker go!

DAVID SEAMAN —— ARSENAL

WHY WAS HE A REJECT? Seaman was heartbroken when he was released after just a year as a professional with Leeds after joining as a schoolboy. He'd made just two appearances for the senior team – both in friendly games – and left the club in tears.

WHAT HAPPENED NEXT? The 'keeper was barely given time to mope. He was offered a chance at Peterborough United, grabbed it with both hands, and began to climb the career ladder, going to Birmingham City and then QPR before Arsenal came knocking.

HAS HE PROVED THEM WRONG? Let's see, Seaman has been England's No.1 'keeper for several years – playing in the 1998 World Cup, Euro '96 and Euro 2000 – so it'd be safe to say yes! He's also had a long, illustrious club career with Arsenal, winning several trophies.

MUZZY IZZET —— LEICESTER CITY

WHY WAS HE A REJECT? A true Londoner hailing from Mile End, Muzzy began his career as a trainee at Chelsea. But the midfielder couldn't get a sniff of first-team action at Stamford Bridge and moved to the Midlands.

WHAT HAPPENED NEXT? Leicester snapped him up on loan in 1996 to boost their chances of promotion to the Premiership. He helped them win the play-off final, became a hero at Filbert Street and a permanent deal followed.

HAS HE PROVED THEM WRONG? Yes and no. Since the move, Izzet has developed into a fine midfielder who's starred as Leicester continue to do well in the Premiership, and he's even been claimed by Turkey to grace the international stage. But whether Chelsea, with their embarrassment of exotic superstars, have missed him is another matter altogether.

NEIL LENNON —— CELTIC

David Seaman had to drop down the divisions before starring in goal for Arsenal and England.

WHY WAS HE A REJECT? Man. City, a club that has been connected with some shocking transfer decisions over the past decade or so, chose to release the midfielder after playing in just one competitive game for the Maine Road outfit. It proved to be a very dubious decision.

WHAT HAPPENED NEXT? Crewe, who are well known for spotting talent, picked him up on a free. Lennon played 147 games for the club before moving to Leicester for £750,000 in 1996 and helping them to the Premiership.

HAS HE PROVED THEM WRONG? Man. City should be cursing the day they let Lennon go. He quickly became one of the most influential players at Leicester, running the team from midfield and being linked with a number of big-money moves, before leaving for Celtic in 2000. City missed out on a diamond.

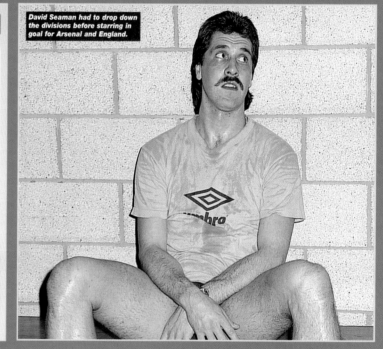

DION DUBLIN —— ASTON VILLA

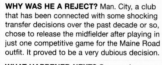

WHY WAS HE A REJECT? A young Dion must have thought he'd struck gold when he was snapped up by Norwich City from lowly Oakham United in 1988. Yet less than five months later he was given a free transfer.

WHAT HAPPENED NEXT? Well, Cambridge United weren't slow to spot Dion's potential and signed him. A flood of goals over four seasons, as The U's achieved successive promotions, was obviously enough to convince Man. United to pay £1 million for his talent!

HAS HE PROVED THEM WRONG? A broken leg severely restricted his United career, but Dion stayed in the top-flight with a move to Coventry. He scored freely there and won England honours before moving to rivals Aston Villa and playing in the 2000 FA Cup Final. Norwich still languish in Division One.

JAMIE CLAPHAM —— IPSWICH TOWN

WHY WAS HE A REJECT? Clapham was signed as a trainee by Tottenham in 1994 but, apart from a solitary substitute's appearance in 1996-97, he couldn't make an impact. The left-back had loan spells at Leyton Orient and Bristol Rovers but was going nowhere fast.

WHAT HAPPENED NEXT? Ipswich drafted him in on a month's loan to cover for injuries in January 1998, but he impressed enough to earn a second month at the club. He signed permanently, for £300,000, in March 1998.

HAS HE PROVED THEM WRONG? Definitely. The fee Ipswich paid Spurs looks like a snip, particularly during last season when Clapham was touted as a possible England player after helping unfancied Town to a great finish in the Premiership. Tottenham could have saved the £5 million they splashed out on Ben Thatcher!

JAMES BEATTIE —— SOUTHAMPTON

WHY WAS HE A REJECT? Beattie was out on the golf course when he took a call from the Blackburn secretary telling him he was being flogged to Southampton as part of the deal which took Kevin Davies to Ewood Park. He'd played just four games for his local club.

WHAT HAPPENED NEXT? The young striker trotted off to The Dell. After an initial struggle for goals, Beattie started banging them in left, right and centre during the 2000-01 season. And they weren't all tap-ins – he scored some spectacular efforts, too. And who was his strike partner? Kevin Davies – spooky, eh?

HAS HE PROVED THEM WRONG? Too right. Considering Davies's failure at Ewood Park, it's fair to say Rovers would have been better off saving £7.5 million and keeping Beattie. The Saints certainly got the better deal.

MALCOLM CHRISTIE - DERBY COUNTY

WHY WAS HE A REJECT? It wasn't so much that Malc was rejected, he was ignored. After scoring a hatful of goals in non-league football he had a trial with his local side Peterborough but wasn't given a second chance to impress.

WHAT HAPPENED NEXT? Christie stuck with his hometown club Deeping Rangers before catching the eye of non-league side Nuneaton Borough. A prolific run there led to his name being bandied around and Christie was soon checked out by Leicester City and Tottenham before Derby pounced for his signature.

HAS HE PROVED THEM WRONG? There are a few Premiership sides now wishing they had listened to the reports of a talented young striker doing the business at Nuneaton, let alone Peterborough. It's still early days, but 'Magic Malc' looks to have an exciting future.

Malcolm Christie failed to impress at a trial with his local club – but he now plays in the Premiership!

CARLO CUDICINI —— CHELSEA

WHY WAS HE A REJECT? Born in the city of Milan, Carlo harboured ambitions of making it with Italian giants AC Milan, but he didn't play a single game in his time at the San Siro.

WHAT HAPPENED NEXT? The 'keeper fared slightly better at smaller Italian clubs Como and Prato, but blew his second big chance at Lazio – making just once appearance before being shipped off to tiny Castel di Sangro. From there, he was loaned out to Chelsea.

HAS HE PROVED THEM WRONG? Blessed as they are with huge squads, neither Milan nor Lazio are likely to be sweating over the loss of Cudicini. However, if the 'keeper can establish himself as Chelsea's No.1 – and he made great progress last season – at least two of Italy's biggest clubs will acknowledge that they should have given Carlo a chance.

SHAY GIVEN —— NEWCASTLE UNITED

WHY WAS HE A REJECT? Irishman Shay was delighted when he was handed a trainee contract at Celtic, but he only lasted a year at Parkhead before being released without even playing for the first team. He joined Blackburn on a free transfer, but only played two games.

WHAT HAPPENED NEXT? Rovers didn't ditch Shay straight away. He was loaned out to Swindon for a short time and then had a spell with Sunderland, where he quickly made a name for himself. The Black Cats wanted to keep him, but bitter rivals Newcastle made a £1.5 million bid in 1997 and that was that.

HAS HE PROVED THEM WRONG? Celtic and Blackburn should be kicking themselves as Shay has not only established himself in the Premiership with The Magpies, but also internationally with the Republic Of Ireland.

SHAUN GOATER —— MANCHESTER CITY

WHY WAS HE A REJECT? Shaun actually began his career, believe it or not, at giants Manchester United. But after spending five months at Old Trafford as a junior player he made the step down to Rotherham United.

WHAT HAPPENED NEXT? Goater spent seven years with Rotherham, during which time he earned a reputation as an entertaining, if unpredictable striker. Still, he moved from there to Bristol City, where his prolific record earned him a £400,000 switch to Maine Road.

HAS HE PROVED THEM WRONG? Well, United have probably never regretted cutting him loose – given the strikers on the books at Old Trafford – but Goater has proved a point. His goals got City promotion and, after a long wait, he achieved his dream of playing in the Premiership in 2000-01, albeit not for long.

Things to do to annoy Villa manager John Gregory!

1 ASK FOR A TRANSFER!
dwight yorke

In 1998, Man. United were chasing Yorkie and he asked to leave Villa. Gregory said he felt like shooting him!

2 SAY YOU'RE DEPRESSED!
stan collymore

Collymore was having such a bad time at Villa he became depressed. Gregory wasn't happy and soon sold him.

3 PLAY UNDER-PAR!
david ginola

Gregory bought Ginola, but wasn't happy with his poor performances and then criticised the Frenchman in the Press.

4 KEEP YOUR MONEY!
doug ellis

Gregory slammed Villa chairman Ellis for not giving him money for a new striker, but then withdrew his remarks.

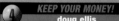

5 MAKE BAD DECISIONS!
any referee

Gregory is well known for bad-mouthing referees when he believes they've made mistakes in a game.

6 PUNISH HIM!
the fa

After his criticism of referees, Gregory was given a touchline ban by the FA in 1999-2000 and he wasn't happy!

7 BE A DIFFICULT AGENT!
you know who you are

Gregory reveals in his autobiography that although he likes some agents, there are others he really can't stand!

8 HAVE A DUBIOUS INJURY!
mark bosnich

Bosnich's transfer saga to Man. United riled Gregory and was made worse when Boz picked up a total non-injury!

9 WIND HIM UP!
ken bates

Before the 2000 FA Cup Final, Chelsea supremo Bates criticised Villa's playing style. It wound Greggers up big time!

10 GO OFF THE RAILS!
lee hendrie

Gregory had to have words with youngster Hendrie when he went off the rails and nearly died in a car crash.

DREAM TEAM

Ashley Cole Arsenal

"I'd have three players in midfield and Zinedine Zidane just in front of them, playing behind the front two strikers. Thierry Henry would be in my team because he has great pace and skill, while Christian Vieri is a great finisher, so I think they'd work well together. Zidane and Vieira are legends – in fact all the midfielders I've chosen are legends! I'd love to play in that back four, but I don't think it'll happen! Those centre-backs would let me get forward and attack more, which is something I like to do."

Cafu — Roma
Position Defender — Country Brazil

Fabio Cannavaro — Parma
Position Defender — Country Italy

Fabien Barthez — Manchester United
Position Goalkeeper — Country France

Tony Adams — Arsenal
Position Defender — Country England

Ashley Cole — Arsenal
Position Defender — Country England

Luis Figo — Real Madrid
Position Midfielder — Country Portugal

Zinedine Zidane — Juventus
Position Midfielder — Country France

Thierry Henry — Arsenal
Position Striker — Country France

Christian Vieri — Inter Milan
Position Striker — Country Italy

David Beckham — Manchester United
Position Midfielder — Country England

Patrick Vieira — Arsenal
Position Midfielder — Country France

REDKNAPP IN CYBERSPACE

Footballers must have loads of free time, right? They train in the morning and then have all afternoon to themselves, so other than buying flash clothes and listening to the coolest music, what do they do? Well, a bunch of footballers have set up their own websites. Liverpool's Jamie Redknapp is one of them and he's even e-mailing fans through the site. "I'm starting to send e-mails now, I'm just getting into it," Jamie told Route 1. "If people want to speak to you, and if you're going to have a website for the fans, it's important to get back to them by replying to their e-mails. If you're going to do it, you've got to do it properly." And rightly so! You can e-mail Jamie via his site at: www.bigfanof.com.

YORKE BEFORE YOU TALK!

If you were as good at footy as Dwight Yorke you wouldn't want people telling you what to do on the pitch, would you? You certainly wouldn't want anyone saying that you, a European Cup winner, still had loads to learn about the beautiful game. Well, actually, the Man. United striker says he still has a lot to learn and welcomes more coaching. "Even at my age, I feel like I'm still learning. I think the day I stop learning is the day that I should retire from the game. There's always something which comes up in games and clicks in your mind, and with experience you hopefully won't make the same mistakes again." So let Dwight teach you a thing or two if you get the chance – you could learn a lot from him!

MATCH ENTERTAINERS

PAOLO DI CANIO
West Ham United

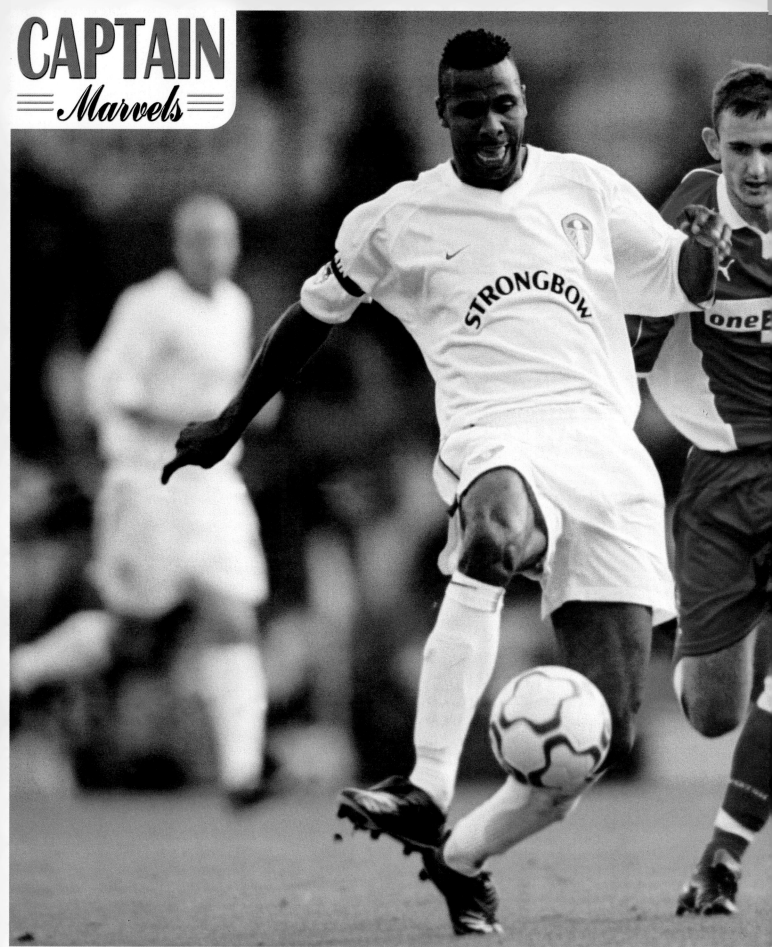

CAPTAIN *Marvels*

LUCAS RADEBE TIMELINE...

JULY
NATIONAL PRIDE
Plays for South Africa as they are re-admitted to world football by FIFA. Plays in the inaugural match, a 2-2 draw against Cameroon

1991

SEPTEMBER
ENGLAND MOVE
Signs for Howard Wilkinson's Leeds for £250,000 and makes his debut against Sheffield Wednesday in a 1-1 draw

1992

DECEMBER
BACK IN THE FRAME
Returns to the Leeds line-up against Bolton in a 2-0 win after eight months out with ligament damage

1993

1994

FEBRUARY
CUP CONQUEROR
Plays a crucial role as South Africa lift the African Nations Cup, beating Tunisia 2-0 in the final

1995

JUNE
CAPTAIN FANTASTIC
Captains South Africa in first World Cup qualifier, winning 1-0 win against Malawi

1996

DECEMBER
STARTING STRIKE
Scores his first goal for South Africa against Uruguay in a 4-3 defeat

1997

LUCAS RADEBE

LUCAS RADEBE HAS BEEN THE rock upon which Leeds's defence has been built. The captain has played a vital part in the club's success in recent seasons, but he always lets his peers take the plaudits for their achievements. As captain, Radebe has shown a fighting spirit and determination often found wanting in today's stars. And he has had just as much drama off the field as on it.

His early life was caught up in the struggle against apartheid in South Africa. He didn't even play any football until his late teens, but Kaizer Chiefs soon saw his potential and signed him up. It was during his days with the club that Radebe's career nearly came to an end. The star was driving when a sniper shot him in the back. The bullet travelled through his body before emerging from his right thigh. Amazingly, he fully recovered and went on to play for South Africa, where he was spotted by the then Leeds manager Howard Wilkinson.

MATCH relives all of the key moments from his career as Leeds and South Africa captain.

> " I've got a great deal of time for him on the field and off it... I wouldn't swap him for anyone in England. Lucas should be set in stone and never allowed to leave. "
>
> DAVID O'LEARY

LUCAS RADEBE FACTFILE

BORN: April 12, 1969 in Johannesburg

NATIONALITY: South African

POSITION: Defender

HEIGHT: 6ft 1ins

WEIGHT: 11st 8lbs

FORMER CLUBS: Kaizer Chiefs

SIGNED: From Kaizer Chiefs for £250,000 on September 5, 1994

LEEDS DEBUT: v Sheffield Wednesday on September 7, 1994

APPOINTED LEEDS CAPTAIN: August 1998

TOTAL LEEDS GAMES/GOALS: 218/3 (August 1998 to March 2001)

TROPHIES WON AS CAPTAIN: None

INTERNATIONAL HONOURS: South Africa 61/1

JANUARY
STRIKE SENSATION
Scores his first ever goal for Leeds against Oxford in the FA Cup as Leeds win 4-0

JULY
WORLD LEADER
Leads South Africa to their first ever World Cup finals in France, but the team doesn't get beyond the group phase

AUGUST
THE CHIEF
Becomes Leeds captain with David Hopkin's place uncertain and Gary Kelly injured

SEPTEMBER
GOAL GLORY
Scores a volley while sitting on the ground in 3-1 victory over Partizan Belgrade

DECEMBER
RUSSIAN ROUTE
Scores 84th-minute goal to secure a 1-0 win against Spartak Moscow, taking Leeds into the UEFA Cup Fourth Round against Roma

DONE DEAL
Signs a new four-year deal after rumours of a big move to Italy

APRIL
EXAMPLE TO ALL
Tries his best but Leeds bow out of the UEFA Cup semis against Galatasaray

MAY
CHAMPIONS LEAGUE
Captains Leeds to third place in the Premiership to secure Champions League football

NOVEMBER
GOOD DEEDS
Receives FIFA Fair Play award for work against racism and his support of a charity for South African children

MARCH
EURO CHALLENGE
Takes Leeds into the Champions League Quarter-Finals, but a knee injury in March ends his campaign

1998   1999   2000   2001

> **We could all learn a thing or two from Lucas Radebe, he's brilliant – a true professional.**
>
> IAN HARTE

1996

JUNE CAPTAINING SOUTH AFRICA FOR THE FIRST TIME

Radebe was made captain of South Africa for France '98. It was a special occasion – the country's first World Cup Finals after a long FIFA exclusion because of the apartheid laws.

"I heard Neil Tovey was stepping down as South Africa skipper, but there were arguments about the captaincy. Some people were saying I would get it, but I didn't believe it until I was given the armband. Being captain gives you the chance to see the other side of football."

1998

JULY GOING TO THE WORLD CUP

As England know only too well, qualifying for the 1998 World Cup was no easy task and South Africa had an equally tough test. Radebe successfully captained his country through the qualifying stages and into the Finals, where they played hosts France Denmark and Saudi Arabia. But two draws and a defeat meant they went home early.

"I remember the last game we played to qualify against Congo at home. The last goal made us so proud. It was scored by Phil Masinga, with his long legs, running 40 yards and then banging it in the top corner. It was absolutely joyful, an amazing feeling. There you were – you'd reached the World Cup and you are the most important people during that month because the World Cup is being broadcast all around the world to millions of people and you are representing South Africa. When we played against the host nation, France, it was an absolutely amazing experience."

1998

AUGUST BECOMING LEEDS CAPTAIN

Radebe returned at the start of the 1998-99 campaign to find that manager George Graham had a new task for him – the Leeds captaincy.

"We went back for pre-season training and George called me into the office and told me I was going to be captain. He said he liked my attitude and that I didn't moan about training! I was speechless, I thought, 'Is he telling me the truth?' But it was a great honour to be made captain of a club like Leeds. I don't remember much about my debut, but walking out and wearing the armband, I got a great reception."

1998

DECEMBER PLEDGING HIS FUTURE TO LEEDS

When George Graham left Leeds for Tottenham in 1998 it posed a difficult problem for the skipper. Should he follow the man who made him captain to London or remain where he was – with the club he loved? When the dust settled at Leeds and David O'Leary finally took over the reigns, one of the Irishman's main priorities was convincing Radebe that he should stay Elland Road.

"My heart was always at Leeds, but I was very close to George, so when he left I was waiting to see who would take over because I didn't know how it would be working with a different person. But I was willing to give it a chance. When David O'Leary took the job I was happy to stay – I was very settled at the club, I'd always felt very welcome, so there was no problem. My heart was in Leeds and I had been here and seen the talent at the club, seen the work going on behind the scenes, and I wanted to be a part of what I knew was going to be very good future."

1999

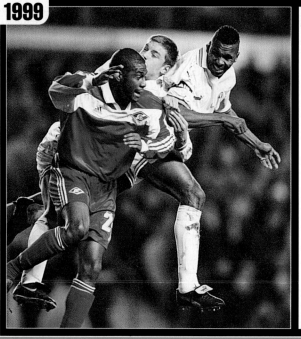

DECEMBER BATTLING FOR GLORY IN THE UEFA CUP

The captain's strong belief that Leeds United were going places proved to be right as the Yorkshire side qualified for Europe in 1998-99. In the following campaign, 1999-2000, the club embarked on an amazing run through to the UEFA Cup semi-finals. Leading the team out against the giants of Italy, Roma, proved a real thrill for the Leeds captain, who scored two rare goals to take The Whites into the last four of the competition.

"One of the best games I had was against Roma. We lost 1-0 away, but it was a real eye-opener, a great experience. To be captain and lead out the team against a side like that was incredible. I scored two goals in that run, my favourite being the one against Spartak Moscow. It was a very important goal because we needed to win and I scored with only five minutes to go. Then there was the goal against Partizan Belgrade, where I scored while on the ground. Not everyone can score goals like that, only people like Romario or Ronaldo! It was funny because a cross came over to the back post and flipped up. I had fallen over but when the ball came down I stuck out my leg and it went in on the volley!"

2000

APRIL COPING WITH TRAGEDY

As Leeds progressed to the UEFA Cup Semi-Finals, a clash with formidable Turkish outfit Galatasaray loomed. But it was in Turkey that triumph turned to disaster before the game even kicked off as two Leeds fans were tragically killed. As news of the events filtered through to the team's hotel, Radebe needed all of his leadership qualities to keep the players together and lead them out in an intimidating stadium.

"Events off the pitch made that game very difficult – especially in Turkey. They were a great side, but it was very hard. We had bad phone calls in the hotel. I was sharing a room with Jason Wilcox and I forgot to take the phone off the hook, so it rang and when I picked it up they said some terrible things. So it was difficult, players are human beings, too and it was really scary. Then, after what happened off the pitch, we still had to play the game but we don't want to make excuses. We didn't play well enough on the night in Turkey and then we couldn't pull the game back in the second game at home."

2000

AUGUST QUALIFYING FOR THE CHAMPIONS LEAGUE

David O'Leary's side had a fantastic 1999-2000 campaign in the Premiership and surprised many so-called experts, considering the amount of young players in the side. On the last day of the season it was down to Leeds and Liverpool for the much-coveted final Champions League place. Leeds hung on for a draw at West Ham while Liverpool fell to plucky Bradford, handing The Whites a qualifying place in Europe's elite competition.

"I was really proud of the team, happy and delighted because it proved that we were heading somewhere. Making it into the Champions League meant we had made a lot of progress and it showed there would be a good future at the club. It was a great result for us to get into the top three – a brilliant season – and we all knew it was going to be good playing in that competition."

2001

JANUARY JUGGLING CAPTAIN'S DUTIES

When you're the respected and well-loved captain of both your club and your country, there will always be a conflict of interests at some point. Radebe nearly quit South Africa because he was unable to combine both his duties.

"It was a problem because I would play for Leeds on Wednesday, fly out to play for South Africa on Saturday and then fly back to play for Leeds on Monday night! It was impossible because I would be tired with all the travelling even though the time difference was only an hour. That's why I had some problems choosing between Leeds and South Africa. Leeds were not at fault and South Africa were not to blame either, it was up to FIFA to sort out a schedule. But now we have come to an agreement."

> **'The Chief' is brilliant. He just cleans everything up at the back. He stops so much coming through and his commitment is fantastic for us.**
>
> PAUL ROBINSON

2001

MARCH GOING FOR CHAMPIONS LEAGUE GLORY

Against all odds, Leeds became a force to be reckoned with in the 2000-01 Champions League. When the groups for the first and second stages were announced, no-one gave them a prayer, but Radebe helped see off the likes of Barcelona and Lazio to make the last eight – putting Leeds back on the European map.

"We knew we weren't just there to make up the numbers. The Champions League features all the big teams and we knew we'd have to play well, but we were enjoying the thought of going to all those amazing places. As captain I had mixed emotions. I was a bit nervous, but excited about playing against the big-names. My favourite moment was the game away at Lazio. We'd played Roma in the UEFA Cup, so we knew what kind of match it'd be. But winning there was a great night for the club – to play in a tie like that and win, and to be part of the celebrations was brilliant."

2001

MAY SUFFERING SEMI-FINAL AGONY

After leading the club through both Champions League phases, Radebe was forced to sit out the semi-final against Valencia after sustaining a knee injury. But his captain's wisdom was still needed, especially when Leeds lost in Spain.

"It was torture! I don't like watching the team out there when I can't play myself. To not play was really disappointing. But the team did very well. Rio Ferdinand and Dominic Matteo came in and did brilliantly, so I was really happy for them. You have to think there'll be a next time. I tried to be a captain off the pitch, that was my duty – to be there for the team. We went out of the competition, but we had to remember that just competing in the Champions League was a great achievement. We played against some great teams and won, and when you think we reached the semi-finals – when Man. United didn't and Barcelona didn't get to the second stage – you've got to be happy with that."

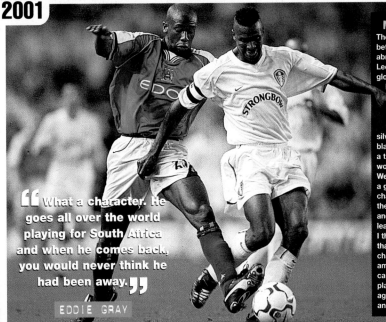

> **What a character. He goes all over the world playing for South Africa and when he comes back, you would never think he had been away.**
>
> EDDIE GRAY

MAY AIMING HIGHER & HIGHER

The years just seem to get better and better for Radebe, both at home and abroad, as he continues to inspire Leeds and South Africa to greater glory. But while there have already been great achievements in his past, Radebe still has big ambitions – and they include lifting trophies as a captain.

"With Leeds I want to win some silverware. I would love to be the first black player from South Africa to lift a trophy in English football – that would go down in the record books. We can only do our very best, but as a group of players we are hungry to challenge for the Premiership title – the atmosphere at the club is brilliant and it would be wonderful to be the league champions. For South Africa, I think we are equipped to do well now that we have stopped chopping and changing the side so much. I have big ambitions for our team. I think being captain of the side makes me a better player and to be captain of my country again at another World Cup would be an incredible experience."

THE FINAL WHISTLE

Remember, you get a point for every correct answer, including every name you find in the Word Spot. Write your answers in the space provided on page 106.

Did Michael Owen score on his Liverpool debut?

third XI

Liverpool dominated English football during the '80s, but just how much do you know about the Merseyside giants?

1 Liverpool captured the European Cup in 1984, but which team did they beat on penalties in the final?

2 Overall, they have won the league 18 times, but when was the last time that The Reds lifted the trophy?

3 Graeme Souness led Liverpool to an FA Cup victory in 1992. Who did they beat 2-0 to win the trophy?

4 Reds hero Robbie Fowler emerged as a first-team regular at Anfield in 1993-94, especially in the League Cup against Fulham. How many goals did the young striker score in that particular game?

5 Fowler eventually scored his first senior England goal in 1996 against which South American side?

6 A classic encounter in April 1996 saw Liverpool beat Newcastle 4-3, but which two Reds stars scored a brace each on that day?

7 Record scorer Ian Rush finally left Liverpool in May 1996. How many goals did the Welshman score for the club and which side did he join after leaving Anfield?

8 True or false? Michael Owen actually scored on his Liverpool debut against Wimbledon in the league.

9 Gerard Houllier became sole manager of The Reds back in 1998. Can you name the joint manager who left?

10 Liverpool signed star striker Emile Heskey in March 2000. How much did they pay Leicester for him?

11 The Reds clinched their UEFA Cup spot on the last day of the 1999-2000 season, despite being beaten 1-0 by which team?

THE MEGA WORD SPOT

Can you spot the international stars from Scotland, Ireland and Wales hiding in the grid below?

S	B	K	W	X	H	A	R	T	E	Q	H	R	Z	H	Z	N	F	Q
H	G	P	D	L	M	H	K	P	O	Z	O	I	N	Z	H	G	L	S
L	Q	O	E	U	A	G	S	V	H	H	V	K	G	P	Q	M	G	L
B	U	R	L	E	Y	X	J	S	U	L	L	I	V	A	N	M	G	B
L	J	I	M	H	O	L	L	A	N	D	I	S	Y	L	L	I	A	D
U	B	E	L	L	A	M	Y	Z	X	R	G	I	G	G	S	Z	T	A
J	O	N	E	S	G	N	A	L	E	L	L	I	O	T	T	U	R	L
S	M	D	G	S	W	O	G	A	L	L	A	C	H	E	R	C	E	L
A	C	I	A	N	G	S	J	O	K	E	N	F	D	E	L	O	B	E
L	A	C	V	T	U	N	R	I	U	E	K	E	A	N	E	N	M	S
G	T	K	A	M	B	I	L	B	V	L	E	R	M	Z	N	N	A	N
U	E	O	S	R	L	B	R	I	H	P	D	G	J	Y	G	O	L	I
O	E	V	M	S	A	O	G	A	S	B	Q	U	I	N	N	L	T	K
D	R	I	D	N	K	R	R	C	R	O	S	S	L	E	Y	L	U	L
Y	J	D	E	C	E	T	R	D	D	D	E	O	Z	J	Q	Y	L	A
P	O	D	N	O	S	I	H	C	T	U	H	N	M	C	C	A	N	N
D	K	M	B	O	Q	O	R	G	C	I	C	A	M	E	R	O	N	X
Y	L	X	N	B	P	Y	R	J	M	D	E	L	A	N	E	Y	X	W
T	N	Q	I	Z	P	O	M	P	O	E	T	T	A	M	D	A	S	J

- BELLAMY
- BLAKE
- BURLEY
- CAMERON
- CONNOLLY
- CROSSLEY
- DAILLY
- DELANEY
- DICKOV
- DODDS
- DOUGLAS
- ELLIOTT
- FERGUSON
- GALLACHER
- GIGGS
- GIVEN
- GOULD
- HARTE
- HARTSON
- HOLLAND
- HUTCHISON
- JONES
- KEANE
- KELLY
- KILBANE
- KINSELLA
- LAMBERT
- MATTEO
- McATEER
- McCANN
- QUINN
- ROBINSON
- SAVAGE
- SPEED
- SULLIVAN

former clubs

Who did these stars play for before their current club?

1 Roy Keane
Manchester United

2 Carl Cort
Newcastle United

3 David Seaman
Arsenal

4 Robbie Keane
Leeds United

5 Kevin Phillips
Sunderland

Who's Missing?

From the England team that triumphed 1-0 over Germany in the group stages of the Euro 2000 Championship?

- SEAMAN
- NEVILLE, G
- ....
- CAMPBELL
- NEVILLE, P
- BECKHAM
- ....
- SCHOLES
- WISE
- SHEARER
- OWEN

1 POINT PER CORRECT ANSWER

MATCH facts CODE BREAKER

CAN YOU SOLVE IT?

To keep his starting XI secret, a football manager has coded the name of his star player. The letters have been turned into numbers, but can you work out who this player is? He could play for any team covered by MATCH facts.

CRACK THE CODE!

21	10	22	25	22

7	2	8	10	23	2	22

THE PLAYER IS...

		A			

	A				

GUESS THE PLAYERS

Three players make up the 'creature' below. Who are they?

1 POINT PER CORRECT ANSWER

DATING AGENCY

Can you guess this player from his personal information?

Nationality: English

Birthplace: Sheffield

Age: 22

Lives: Manchester

Height: 6ft 3ins

Hair: Short and brown

Interests: Becoming England's No.1

1 POINT FOR CORRECT ANSWER

ZINEDINE ZIDANE
France

MATCH
ENTERTAINERS

GLAND XI....EVER?

With the help of experts and fans, **MATCH** presents the contenders for the greatest England team ever.

ATTEMPTING TO FIND THE GREATEST ENGLAND team ever will never be an easy task. The staff at MATCH just couldn't agree on the final XI, so we enlisted the help of a large panel of experts and fans. They had a lot to consider, because football has changed dramatically over the last 100 years – goalkeepers, for example, have only worn gloves in the last 30 years and used to be pushed into the net by opposing strikers!

Then there was the dilemma of comparing the legends of yesteryear with the superstars of today. How would Michael Owen and David Beckham cope wearing clompy old boots and shorts down to their ankles? With all of the votes in, even some of England's 'greats' didn't make the team – David Seaman, Jack Charlton, Tony Adams, David Platt and Kevin Keegan all failed to make the grade.

The most popular players were undoubtedly Stuart Pearce, Bobby Moore and Gary Lineker, while the positions in midfield were the most hotly-contested. Personal battles occurred all over the pitch – Gordon Banks versus Peter Shilton, Sir Stanley Matthews versus David Beckham and Jimmy Greaves versus Geoff Hurst. In many of the positions it was neck-and-neck to decide who would make the final cut. Selection problems occurred at right-back though, where the likes of 1966 World Cup hero George Cohen, ex-Manchester United star Paul Parker and Gary Neville all received nominations.

Over the next six pages, MATCH brings you the final verdict of the panel, plus the best England manager ever, the most capped players and the record goalscorers. But we want to hear your opinions too, so write to MATCH at the address in the front of the annual and tell us who would make your greatest England team ever.

ENGLAND'S RECORD CAP HOLDERS

1.	Peter Shilton (goalkeeper)	125 caps
2.	Bobby Moore (centre-back)	108 caps
3.	Bobby Charlton (midfielder)	106 caps
4.	Billy Wright (centre-back)	105 caps
5.	Bryan Robson (midfielder)	90 caps
6.	Kenny Sansom (left-back)	86 caps
7.	Ray Wilkins (midfielder)	84 caps
8.	Gary Lineker (striker)	80 caps
9.	John Barnes (midfielder)	79 caps
10.	Stuart Pearce (left-back)	78 caps

MANAGERS

Walter Winterbottom was the first of England's 11 managers but only succeeded in creating a national coaching structure. Joe Mercer, Ron Greenwood and Don Revie had mixed spells but failed to lift any silverware. **Bobby Robson** was a big success, taking England to the quarter-finals of the 1986 World Cup and within a penalty kick of the 1990 World Cup final. **Terry Venables** also gave the country some cheer at Euro '96 – after Graham Taylor's dismal reign – but lost in the semi-finals, again on penalties. Kevin Keegan and Glenn Hoddle tried and failed, while it is too early to judge the current boss Sven Goran Eriksson. **Sir Alf Ramsey** is the only manager to win a trophy with England, the 1966 World Cup, so he would be the obvious man to lead out England's Greatest XI.

ENGLAND MANAGERS 1946-2001	
Walter Winterbottom	1946-1962
Sir Alf Ramsey	1963-1974
Joe Mercer	1974
Don Revie	1974-1977
Ron Greenwood	1977-1982
Bobby Robson	1982-1990
Graham Taylor	1990-1993
Terry Venables	1994-1996
Glenn Hoddle	1996-1999
Howard Wilkinson (temporary)	1999 & 2000
Kevin Keegan	1999-2000
Peter Taylor (temporary)	2000
Sven Goran Eriksson	2000-present

CAPTAINS

The most obvious choice for captain of the side is West Ham legend **Bobby Moore**, but he has more than a couple of rivals. Fellow centre–back Billy Wright won 105 caps for England, leading his country out 90 times and proving a dependable and confident skipper. **Bryan Robson** also captained the side by example, demanding 100 per cent effort from his team mates. Many other England favourites have worn the skipper's armband, including **Alf Ramsey**, Kevin Keegan, Jimmy Armfield, Peter Shilton, Gary Lineker, Stuart Pearce, Tony Adams and **Alan Shearer**. But Bobby Moore was the undisputed choice of our panel. The captain of England's 1966 triumph and skipper in 91 of his 108 internationals was coolness personified and would have graced any team in the world.

GOALKEEPERS

England have been spoilt for choice when it comes to the No. 1 jersey over the years and some of the best club 'keepers have failed to pick up more than a handful of international caps. **David Seaman** has made the position his own in the last ten years, providing a commanding presence at the back and making crucial saves, particularly at Euro '96 when he was at his best. But the panel was split between two goalkeepers of the highest quality – **Gordon Banks** and **Peter Shilton**. Banks played a starring role in 1966 when England lifted the World Cup but was forced to end his glorious ten-year international career after a car accident in which he lost an eye. Banks's young understudy at Leicester, **Peter Shilton**, took his place in the national team and made 125 appearances for his country – a record that will be very hard to beat. Shilton won the last of his caps when he was 41 years old and many people believe that he is the greatest goalkeeper England has ever produced.

DEFENDERS

Tony Adams was the last in a long line of defenders to play a starring role for England. **Billy Wright** was captain between 1946-1959 and one of the best defenders in the world. Jimmy Armfield continued the tradition and was voted the best right-back in the world after the 1962 World Cup. **Bobby Moore** is undoubtedly the most famous English defender ever after he won the 1966 World Cup Final next to **Jack Charlton**, Ray Wilson and George Cohen in defence. Roy McFarland, Phil Neal and Emlyn Hughes followed in the '70s, with Terry Butcher, Phil Thompson and Kenny Sansom starring in the '80s. Finally, Stuart Pearce became a hero in the '90s for his commitment and strong tackling. He also exorcised the demons of previously missed penalties by rifling home a spot-kick at Euro '96.

STRIKERS

There are only two places to fight for up front in the 4-4-2 system, but there's a lot of competition. Stan Mortensen and **Wilf Mannion** were the stars of the '40s, while Jackie Milburn and Nat Lofthouse were the leading forwards in the '50s. Sir Alf Ramsey used three men up front in the 1966 World Cup Final – **Geoff Hurst**, Martin Peters and Roger Hunt. Jimmy Greaves was left out of that final but was one of the finest strikers ever to wear The Three Lions. **Kevin Keegan** was the outstanding England frontman of the '70s, while Gary Lineker and Peter Beardsley had a lethal partnership in the '80s. Alan Shearer captained the side at France '98 and Euro 2000 while **Michael Owen** has already proved his goalscoring ability. Picking two strikers from this list of greats was very difficult.

MIDFIELDERS

Our panel had a difficult time choosing just four midfielders from a wealth of talent. Sir Stanley Matthews was the first entertainer the national team ever produced although team mate **Tom Finney** scored more goals. The 1966 trio of Alan Ball, Nobby Stiles and Bobby Charlton were an awesome combination in England's midfield while players like **Trevor Brooking** and Steve Coppell provided the flair in the '70s. Glenn Hoddle, Chris Waddle and John Barnes skipped past defenders in the '80s, **Bryan Robson** captained the side in the 1986 and 1990 World Cups and Paul Gascoigne was the undisputed star of the 1990 tournament. In recent times, Paul Scholes has inherited David Platt's knack of scoring vital goals and current skipper **David Beckham** is one of the finest midfielders in the world.

ENGLAND'S RECORD GOALSCORERS		
1. Bobby Charlton	106 games/49 goals	
2. Gary Lineker		80/48
3. Jimmy Greaves		57/44
4. Nat Lofthouse		33/30
= Alan Shearer		63/30
= Tom Finney		76/30
7. David Platt		62/27
8. Bryan Robson		90/26
9. Geoff Hurst		49/24
10. Stan Mortensen		25/23

SIR BOBBY CHARLTON (1958-1970)
LEFT MIDFIELD 106 caps, 49 goals

Charlton was one of the panel's most popular choices, an instrumental member of England's glorious 1966 team who played in three World Cups. He notched up a phenomenal strike rate from an advanced midfield role – scoring 49 goals in 106 appearances – and terrified the opposition with his trademark cannonball shots from outside the area. Sir Bobby is one of the most respected figures in world football and remains England's record goalscorer.

ALSO IN THE FRAME...

Tom Finney (1946-1959)

76 caps, 30 goals

Preston hot-shot and supremely talented winger.

JIMMY ARMFIELD (1959-1966)
RIGHT-BACK 43 caps, 0 goals

The right-back slot was one of the most hotly-contested positions for England's greatest XI ever but the inclusion of Jimmy Armfield is only a surprise to those who never saw him play. The Blackpool full-back was rock solid in a back four but had an adventurous attacking spirit that was unique in defenders of his generation. Indeed, after the 1962 World Cup Armfield was voted the best right-back in the world. He captained England 14 times before Bobby Moore took over the armband in 1964.

ALSO IN THE FRAME...

George Cohen (1964-1967)

37 caps, 0 goals

Hard-working Fulham defender and 1966 hero.

TERRY BUTCHER (1980-1990)
CENTRE-BACK 77 caps, 3 goals

One of the most committed players ever to pull on an England shirt, Butcher was instrumental in the team's progress in the 1986 and 1990 World Cup finals. The Ipswich centre-back broke a leg before the 1988 European Championships and his country missed him desperately. 'Butch' is best remembered for playing on against Sweden in 1990 despite suffering a deep head wound which left his England shirt covered in blood.

ALSO IN THE FRAME...

Billy Wright (1946-1959)

105 caps, 3 goals

Illustrious England captain in the '40s and '50s.

PAUL GASCOIGNE (1988-1998)
CENTRE MIDFIELD 57 caps, 10 goals

The most talented Englishman of his generation, Gazza was the Player Of The Tournament at the 1990 World Cup aged just 23. On the pitch he excelled at running rings past the opposition, providing vital assists for his team-mates and often scoring himself from mazy runs or brilliant free-kicks. His England career suffered from injury but he came back to star at Euro '96 and played the last game for his country against Belgium two years later. Sadly, England have not found a player to replace him ever since.

ALSO IN THE FRAME...

David Platt (1989-1996)

62 caps, 27 goals

Brilliant goalscoring midfielder during the '90s.

JIMMY GREAVES (1959-1967)
STRIKER 57 caps, 44 goals

Jimmy Greaves is recognised as the greatest natural striker England has ever produced and only Robbie Fowler has been compared to him since his last international appearance in 1967. After leading the line in the early rounds of the 1966 World Cup, Greavsie lost his place in the team to Geoff Hurst because of injury and was not selected to play in the final. Nevertheless, he still has an awesome goalscoring record for his country with 44 goals in 57 internationals.

ALSO IN THE FRAME...

Geoff Hurst (1966-1972)

49 caps, 24 goals

Scored a hat-trick in the 1966 World Cup Final.

BOBBY MOORE (1962-1973)
CENTRE-BACK 108 caps, 2 goals

The best defender England has ever produced. Moore read the game superbly at centre-back, intercepted passes, made supremely-timed tackles and distributed the ball with style. After being completely marked out of the game in the 1970 World Cup, Brazil's legendary striker Pelé called Moore the best defender in the world. The West Ham legend was named Player Of The Tournament at the 1966 World Cup after he captained England to glory at Wembley.

ALSO IN THE FRAME...

Jackie Charlton (1965-1970)

35 caps, 6 goals

Towering Leeds United defender and 1966 hero.

GORDON BANKS (1963-1972)
GOALKEEPER 73 caps, 0 goals

Banksie narrowly beat Peter Shilton to the No. 1 jersey in MATCH's Greatest England Team Ever. He is best known for his incredible save from Pelé during the 1970 World Cup – leaping to his right to push the Brazilian's goal-bound header over the bar. But this wasn't the only occasion that world-class strikers were left holding their heads in astonishment at the Leicester 'stopper. Banks was arguably the finest goalkeeper of his generation and his outstanding reflexes helped England to win the World Cup in 1966.

ALSO IN THE FRAME...

Peter Shilton (1970-1990)

125 caps, 0 goals

Record caps holder and world-class goalkeeper.

GARY LINEKER (1984-1992)
STRIKER 80 caps, 48 goals

Many great strikers have worn the Three Lions, but Gary Lineker comes second only to Bobby Charlton in the most important statistic of them all – scoring goals. Lineker was substituted in his last game for England, denying the forward the chance to equal or even surpass Charlton's all-time goalscoring record. Nevertheless, the Everton, Barcelona and Tottenham striker had a brilliant awareness in the penalty area and was the top scorer in the 1986 World Cup.

ALSO IN THE FRAME...

Nat Lofthouse (1950-1958)

33 caps, 30 games

Bolton striker with an incredible scoring record.

STUART PEARCE (1987-1978)
LEFT-BACK 78 caps, 5 goals

Pearce edged past Kenny Sansom and 1966 World Cup winner Ray Wilson in the eyes of our panel because of his sheer commitment to the cause and the passion he displayed throughout his England career. Another natural leader, he was stronger than any opponent in the tackle and posed plenty of problems to the opposition from dead-ball situations. 'Pyscho' is probably best remembered for his salute to the Wembley crowd after crashing home a spot-kick against Spain at Euro '96 following his missed penalty in the semi-final of the 1990 World Cup.

ALSO IN THE FRAME...

Kenny Sansom (1979-1988)

86 caps, 1 goal

England's most capped full-back of all-time.

SIR STANLEY MATTHEWS (1934-1957)
RIGHT MIDFIELD 54 caps, 3 goals

Widely regarded as the best dribbler ever seen in English football, Matthews made his England debut aged 19 and played his last game for his country at 42. The 'Wizard of Dribble' combined with fellow winger Tom Finney to strike fear into international defences by turning them inside out before setting up grateful team-mates. Sir Stanley remains the only footballer ever to be awarded a knighthood while still playing.

ALSO IN THE FRAME...

David Beckham (1996-present)

41 caps, 3 goals

Man. United star set to be an England legend.

BRYAN ROBSON (1980-1991)
CENTRE MIDFIELD 90 caps, 26 goals

Captain Marvel, as he was known, was probably the most complete midfielder England has ever produced. Robson was a natural leader with a brilliant engine that allowed him to protect his defence, win the ball with crunching tackles and make surging runs into the opposition's box. He also scored some important goals for England, ending his international career with 26 strikes in 90 appearances. Despite injury problems, many of them caused by his legendary bravery in the tackle, Robbo captained England 65 times.

ALSO IN THE FRAME...

Alan Ball (1965-1975)

72 caps, 8 goals

Midfield battler – won 1966 World Cup aged 21.

FOOTY MAD!

THEY SAID WHAT!

MATCH looks back at some of the gems we overheard last season…

"I was conscious when my knee was operated upon. And when I saw the new ligament coming into the theatre I thought, 'This is what I came here for. This is the start of my comeback and my chance for a second career'." Dutch striker Ruud van Nistelrooy talks about the operation to repair a ligament which saw the postponement of his £19 million move from PSV Eindhoven to Manchester United.

"They've kissed and made up now. But I know whose side I'd be on in a row, that's for sure." Leicester manager Peter Taylor gangs up in Ged Taggart's corner after the defender has a scuffle on the field with his team-mate Robbie Savage. We know whose side we'd be on too – sorry Sav!

"It doesn't matter that this match was not at Wembley – it could've been in my mate's back garden. All that matters is we won." A jubilant Robbie Fowler after Liverpool won the Worthington Cup final at the Millennium Stadium in Cardiff. For the record, his mate's back garden failed a pitch inspection.

"The Goal Of The Month has been disallowed. I can't remember seeing such a goal disallowed, not even in 'Roy Of The Rovers'." The Manchester City manager Joe Royle talks comically after Danny Tiatto's spectacular goal against Middlesbrough was disallowed in the 1-1 draw at The Riverside.

"He has all those, 'Go on my son, get stuck in' clichés in his locker." Striker Dennis Bergkamp reveals the tactical side of Arsenal's French manager Arsene Wenger in the Highbury dressing room.

"Yes, I was surprised. But I've always said nothing surprises me in football." Spurs frontman Les Ferdinand, when asked whether he was surprised when he heard of George Graham's shock sacking at White Hart Lane.

"I will dance around in my lederhosen if we beat United." Bayern Munich captain Steffen Effenberg gets a little bit too patriotic before the German giants play Manchester United in the quarter-finals of the Champions League. We've yet to see the pictures of his merry jig!

Taking defeat lying down is not always a good idea.

Having to wash your own kit can be very upsetting!

"Er, Michael, it was offside and now they're attacking... doh!"

"How many times? I hate being called Celine!" says Dion.

Michael did it all on his 'Owen' against Roma.

Barcelona are awarded a throw-in at Liverpool.

"Who wants to swap a shirt for me big black overcoat?"

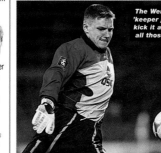
The Werder Bremen 'keeper just couldn't kick it after scoffing all those meat pies!

"The season's over, thank goodness!"

Ian Harte celebrates yet another 40-yard tap-in.

"So your head is like a twist-off bottle cap, no?"

1860 Munich coach Werner Lorant volunteers for a Kevin Keegan impersonation night.

Thierry rises like a salmon and stings like an Henry!

The Anfield piggyback race is won by Carragher and Barmby.

"Robbo, gottle-a geer, eh? Bottle of... sorry Bryan!"

Scott Parker's just heard he's got chips for tea...

...but chuffed PSG boss Luis Fernandes got to them first!

Michael Carrick goes head over heels when West Ham seal a win.

Smicer shows off his chess moves. That's Czech mate!

Rivaldo shows just how hungry he is at Barca.

Spurs hear of George Graham's sacking.

Freddie Ljungberg's latest hair colour was obviously too embarrassing for him!

"Why you book-a me ref? It was-a Carrick who jumped on me!"

MATCH
ENTERTAINERS

FANCY DANS!

LES FERDINAND tells **MATCH** why footballers have such flashy reputations and we reveal the fancy dans of the Premiership!

YESTERDAY'S GENERATION OF FOOTBALLERS WERE A MOTLEY CREW WITH THEIR SHELL SUITS AND trainers. In the '60s it was Bobby Moore and his sensible suits, while the main fashion in the '70s was Kevin Keegan's mop-top perm – enough said! It's different for today's stars, who are more like pop stars with their designer clothes, loads of money and fan worship – they're seriously flash!

Today's footballers model for fashion designers, advertise shampoo and go to movie premieres and celebrity parties. Some even have the ultimate accessory – a pop star girlfriend or model wife! They wake up in country mansions or posh city apartments and once training is over they'll drive to the shops in an expensive motor – take your pick from Ferraris, Porsches, Jeeps and many more.

Tottenham striker Les Ferdinand loves his cars, so he took MATCH on a test-drive to explain why footballers have earned 'fancy dan' reputations. And over the page, we reveal some of the flashiest players in the Premiership – as nominated by their long-suffering team mates!

LES, WE'VE HEARD YOU'VE GOT A PASSION FOR CARS?

"I do like cars. People always say I don't keep them for long enough, but I enjoy driving a lot. I pretty much drive everywhere I go – I've always had quite fast cars, in fact I'm a bit of a speed freak! I've had Porsches, a Ferrari 550 and a Ferrari 360 Medina, which was probably my favourite. I've also had a Mercedes 4.3a MG – they're all fast cars and I've enjoyed driving all of them."

IT'S TYPICAL FOR FOOTBALLERS TO HAVE NICE CARS ISN'T IT?

"Yeah, I think it probably is a typical footballer's thing. What I'd say is 95 per cent of footballers come from working-class backgrounds and they'd never usually get the chance to drive a Ferrari or a Porsche if they weren't a footballer. When you're a kid you always say, 'I'm going to buy a Porsche when I'm older' and as a footballer you're able to realise that dream."

ARE ALL FOOTBALLERS FLASHY?

"I think the stereotype is made by other people. I was driving my dad's car, a Ford Focus, one day and I pulled up at a garage to put some petrol in. This guy

recognised me and came over. He said, 'What are you doing driving this?' So I just explained that I liked it. He said, 'I thought you'd have something like a Porsche or a Ferrari'. I didn't tell him that I did actually own those models – I just said I enjoyed driving the car and that I was happy with it. But he expected me to drive something better, so I think it's people's expectations. People expect professional footballers to have fast cars, big houses and model girlfriends."

DO YOU THINK BEING FLASHY IS A BAD THING?

"No, a lot of people say that footballers are flash, but if you put those people in the same situation, they'd do exactly the same thing. I think there probably is an expectation there though and I must admit, some footballers probably try to live up to that."

ARE THERE SOME NICE CARS IN THE TOTTENHAM CAR PARK THEN?

"There are some nice cars, yeah! A lot of the players are into Range Rovers at the moment, so there's a few of those. There's an array of other nice cars in there, but I won't tell you if I think mine is the best!"

> **"PEOPLE EXPECT FOOTBALLERS TO HAVE FAST CARS, BIG HOUSES AND MODEL GIRLFRIENDS."**

LEEDS UNITED

WHO: OLIVIER DACOURT

NOMINATED BY: OLIVIER DACOURT

WHY? "If it is down to the player who loves his cars and his clothes the most, I would have to think for a bit before saying… it is me! I don't think I'm a terrible poser or a big head but I do like to dress well and try to look fashionable. Maybe it's because I am French and we are renowned as a nation of trendy people! But if you were asking me who is the worst at looking good, I'd have to say our right-back Gary Kelly! He's an awful dresser! I wouldn't want to swap clothes with him – that's for sure."

SUNDERLAND

WHO? MICHAEL GRAY

NOMINATED BY: DANNY DICHIO

WHY? "People might think I'm flashy but it's not true. Our captain Mickey Gray thinks he's flashy, but none of the other lads think he is! He wears the worst pair of jeans I've ever seen – they look like they belong to his grandad or something. They look like they've just had paint splattered all over them. He thinks they're fashionable, but all the lads think he's been doing painting and decorating before he comes into training in the mornings! He bought himself a brand new Ferrari two seasons ago, so he's probably got the best car at the club as well!"

SOUTHAMPTON

WHO? JAMES BEATTIE & MATT OAKLEY

NOMINATED BY: PAUL JONES

WHY? "There are two main flashy players at Southampton. James Beattie has a Porsche and he always wears designer clothes. He's young and good-looking, so I'm sure he gets a lot of attention from the ladies! Matty Oakley now drives an Aston Martin DB7 and he's also a good-looking guy. They both got a bit of stick from the other players when they first bought their cars, but we've laid off them now. When I was that age and just starting out in football I used to knock around in an old Vauxhall!"

DERBY COUNTY

WHO? DEON BURTON

NOMINATED BY: DARRYL POWELL

WHY? "Deon's a nightmare! He's got to have a label on everything. He was into Prada big style and everything had to be made by Prada. Prada shoes, trousers – some crap ones as well! He likes Luis Vuitton stuff as well – all the luggage sets. You just look at him and think, 'What's he up to with that girly Louis Vuitton bag?' He's not too bad with cars, but he does change them regularly. He does like something nice to drive, but then don't we all?"

NEWCASTLE UNITED

WHO? KIERON DYER

NOMINATED BY: SHOLA AMEOBI

WHY? "Kieron's not really all that flashy – he just knows the sort of thing he likes. He likes nice things, but then we all do, don't we? He's quite big on his jewellery and then he sometimes gets designer clothes. He crashed his nice car though, his Mercedes, but fortunately he was all right. Nobody takes the mickey out of him too much, we just let him get on with it. To be honest, he's not really any worse than anyone else at the club, but that's the thing about being in football – it means you can afford to buy nice things now and again if you want to."

BLACKBURN ROVERS

WHO? DAVID DUNN

NOMINATED BY: MATT JANSEN

WHY? "That's Dunny – David Dunn, without a doubt. He's just streaked his hair, he's got short dark hair and he's had highlights in it so he looks like a pint of Guinness now! He used to have this really short hair but he's grown it and had yellow bits put in! He's also got a very flash car. But he banged it just after he bought it and it cost him something like £2,000 to get it fixed, so he wasn't very happy when that happened!"

CHELSEA

WHO? JODY MORRIS

NOMINATED BY: GRAEME LE SAUX

WHY? "It's definitely not me! There is no-one in particular who is flash at Chelsea, but there are fashion conscious players. Jody Morris is very into his fashion. But I'd like to think everyone at the club is fashion conscious because of the image of the club and the fact that we're just off the Kings Road! The big rage in the car park at the moment are the BMW X5s – there are about seven of them at the club. A couple of players have Ferraris and that's quite flash from my point of view – I never park next to them!"

LEICESTER CITY

WHO? ROBBIE SAVAGE

NOMINATED BY: STEVE GUPPY

WHY? "Without doubt, the flashiest player at Leicester is Robbie Savage. He really does take pride in his appearance and he spends a lot of money on the way he looks. He always wears the top designer labels and he likes to go out a lot so everyone can see how good he looks! The lads at Leicester have got their own theory as to why he always looks well dressed – we reckon his girlfriend picks out all his clothes for him! He looks good, but all the lads take the mickey out of him in plenty of other ways to make up for it! He drives a Porsche as well, so he has got the car to match his clothes!"

VINNIE JONES

AGONY AUNT

The Hollywood hard man of footy offers his advice to the game's stars!

HAIR SCARE!

Dear Vinnie,
I've taken some stick over haircuts, not to mention facial hair. But nobody told me a simple ponytail would be an object of derision! He, he, he. I really need some advice about what kind of look I can go for. I haven't got a clue about fashion.
David, North London

VINNIE SAYS: "Whatcha going on abaaat? It's simple enough, pop down to yer barbers and tell the geezer you want a number one all over. Vwaa-lah! You've got yerself the look that all footy players are getting now. Simple and hard!"

RETIREMENT!

Dear Vinnie,
I'm heading for retirement but I've got fears about what I can dae after I quit the rat race. I've always been a successful wee fella but I'm not gonnae have any way of competing except for watching 'Countdown' with mae wife and playing a round of golf.
Alex, Manchester

VINNIE SAYS: "Easy my saan. You ever trained greyhaands? Well, that's the life fer you! You got some moolah, ain't 'cha? Well buy a load from a good litter and bring 'em up racing against eachuvver. They'll soon come good and you'll be back competing again. Laaaverly."

LANGUAGE WORRY!

Caro Vincenzo,
sono cos infelice. Non posso farsi capito qui in Inghilterra perch non parlo il linguaggio e molto sta frustrando per me. Quando provo a parlare inglese. Potete aiutare?
Claudio, ad ovest Londra

VINNIE SAYS: "What the blaaady...?!? Yer talkin' foreign ter me mate – you need ter take some English lessons my saan!"

THE Numbers GAME

SPOTLIGHT ON: WHITE HART LANE

748	91	3,500	4,200,000
The number of the Red House on High Road where Tottenham's first HQ was set up. This was more glamorous than former meeting places, which varied from the YMCA to under a lamppost!	The amount of years since the symbol of a cockerel on a ball was added to the West Stand. It is now on the East Stand and, as a time capsule, apparently holds a 1908 acceptance letter to the league.	This is the amount of soil in tons which was deposited on Hackney Marsh to help the drainage of the White Hart Lane pitch in 1952. A new filter system was then installed with 1.5 miles of drains.	This was the total cost in pounds of the club's new West Stand, which became the most expensive stand in Britain at the time. It took 13 months to complete and was finished in February 1982.

75,038	2	1,000	8,030
Tottenham's record attendance at White Hart Lane came in the sixth round of the FA Cup on March 5, 1938. Sadly, for all the fans who packed out the ground, Spurs lost 1-0 to visitors Sunderland!	The club introduced two close-circuit cameras in 1985 to film events inside the ground on matchdays. There are 11 additional cameras used to monitor the streets surrounding the stadium.	The club was made to guarantee to its landlords, Charrington Breweries, that this number of fans would turn up for matches to cover the rent on the site, which became White Hart Lane.	This is the precise measurement of the Spurs pitch in square yards. Ironically, this is exactly the same size as Arsenal's pitch, despite claims that the playing surface at Highbury is much smaller!

ENGLISH BOYS HAVE MORE FUN!

Want to know why there are so many stars coming over from Italy's Serie A to play in the Premiership, while so few English players are going in the opposite direction? Well, according to Middlesbrough's fun-loving Aussie, Paul Okon – who played in Italy with Fiorentina prior to coming to England – it's all linked to having a good time! **"Playing football in Italy is very different to what I've experienced in England,"** Paul told Route 1. **"The kind of pressure that surrounds the game over there is enormous. The newspapers and television control football in Italy and that takes the fun out of it."** Wow! And if a Middlesbrough player says England's more fun, Italy must be bad!

ASHLEY'S EASY LIFE!

If you think Arsenal's young star Ashley Cole looks a little too relaxed for comfort, there's actually a good reason for it – his old-man team-mates Dave Seaman, Tony Adams, Lee Dixon and Martin Keown! Despite breaking into a defence that contained a few players old enough to be his dad, Cole was given the easy life, as he explained to Route 1. **"They all made it easy for me, even training with them,"** he recalled, wistfully. **"And when I played next to them, they made it even easier for me because of their experience. They always knew what to do and they helped me out a lot!"** And in return, the promising left-back was always on hand with the Horlicks. Good lad, Ash!

RESPECT SUNDERLAND!

Oi, give Sunderland a bit of credit, will yer? Super Kevin Phillips is fed up of The Black Cats getting no praise for their achievements in the Premiership, so you'd better start giving them some respect! Wanna know why they're so good? Well, let the striker explain! **"A major factor that has shone through is our team spirit, it's our togetherness,"** Kev told his mates at Route 1. **"It's been like that ever since I joined the club. Peter Reid has added to the squad to make it a lot stronger and we can play as well. Some people think we're just a hard-working side, but we play some good football and we're always looking to score goals. We're definitely a tough side to beat."** Not to mention the fact that you've got Scottish hard-man Alex Rae in yer midfield. Now he is tough – Peter Reid must be so proud of him!

HENRIK LARSSON

Celtic

CAPTAIN *Marvels*

TONY ADAMS TIMELINE...

NOVEMBER
STARTING OUT
Joins Arsenal on schoolboy forms

1980

APRIL
SIGNING ON
Becomes an apprentice at Arsenal

1981

NOVEMBER
FIRST-TEAMER
Makes senior team debut in the 2-1 home defeat by Sunderland

1982

JANUARY
PRO FORMS
Signs professional forms for Arsenal

1983

FEBRUARY
ENGLAND DEBUT
Makes his senior bow for England in 4-2 win over Spain in Madrid

1984

1985

MAY
TOP YOUNG GUN
Named PFA Young Player Of The Year

1986

MARCH
LEADER
Takes over the Arsenal captaincy from Kenny Sansom

1987

MAY
CUP UPSET
Captains Arsenal to League Cup Final but loses out to Luton at Wembley

1988

JUNE
DONKEY TAG
Newspapers nicknames him 'donkey' after a poor display at Euro '88 with England

1989

MAY
TITLE GLORY
Lifts league title with Arsenal after beating Liverpool on last day of 1990 season

1990

JUNE
LEFT OUT
Misses the World Cup after being left out of Bobby Robson's England squad

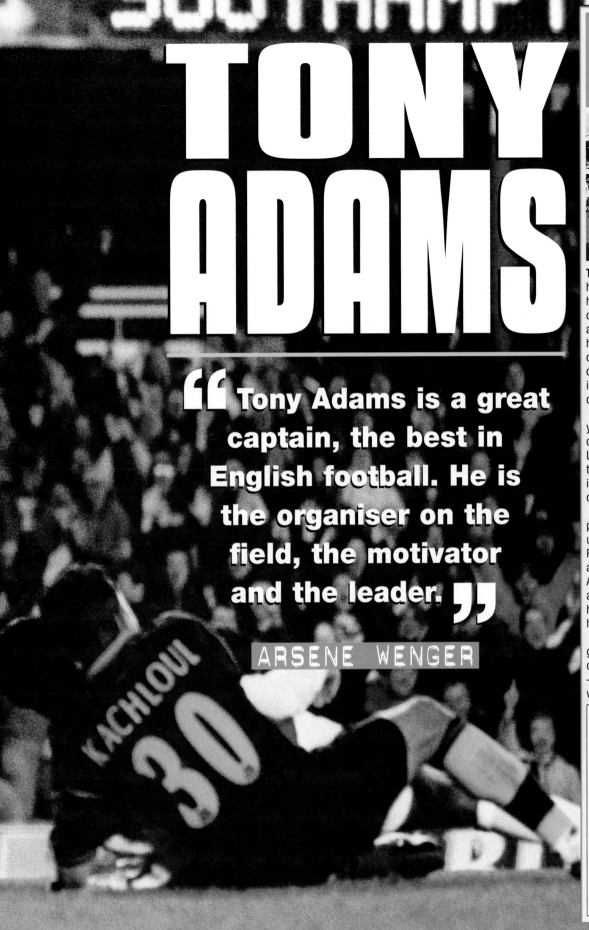

TONY ADAMS

> **"Tony Adams is a great captain, the best in English football. He is the organiser on the field, the motivator and the leader."**
>
> ARSENE WENGER

TONY ADAMS HAS LONG BEEN hailed as a born leader. But even he was surprised to be named captain of Arsenal at the tender age of 21. Not that this worried him – he first wore the armband on New Year's Day 1988, when club skipper Kenny Sansom was injured, and was made the new captain within three months.

Weeks later, the commanding young defender led The Gunners out of the tunnel for the 1988 League Cup Final at Wembley – the first of his many appearances in the famous stadium as a proud captain of both club and country.

Thirteen years on, Adams's presence in defence remains unparalleled in English football. Representing a tower of strength and authority, he is idolised by Arsenal supporters but is surely a nemesis to every striker who has ever been thwarted by one of his well-timed crunching tackles.

MATCH looks back at the glorious career of the Arsenal captain and ex-England skipper – a glorious 20-year tenure in which he's seen and done it all.

TONY ADAMS FACTFILE

BORN:	October 10, 1966 in Romford
NATIONALITY:	English
POSITION:	Defence
HEIGHT:	6ft 3in
WEIGHT:	13st 9lbs
FORMER CLUBS:	None
SIGNED:	From youth on January 30, 1984
ARSENAL DEBUT:	v Sunderland on November 5, 1983
APPOINTED CAPTAIN:	March 1989
TOTAL ARSENAL GAMES/GOALS:	660/48 (March 1989 to May 2001)
TROPHIES WON AS CAPTAIN:	1989 & 1991 Division One (old), 1993 FA Cup & League Cup, 1994 European Cup-Winners' Cup, 1998 Premier League, 1998 FA Cup
INTERNATIONAL HONOURS:	England 66/5, England B, Under-21, Youth

---

MAY
DEFENSIVE ROCK
Lets in only 18 goals all season as part of a legendary defence to capture a second league championship
1991

MAY
OUT OF FAVOUR
Misses out on the England squad for Euro '92 in Sweden
1992

CUP DOUBLE
Helps The Gunners to a domestic cup double by beating Sheff. Wed in both cup finals
1993

APRIL/MAY
EURO STAR
Leads Arsenal to European Cup-Winners' Cup triumph over Parma
1994

MAY
CUP MISERY
Loses 2-1 to Real Zaragoza in the 1994 European Cup-Winners' Cup Final
1995

1996

JUNE
LIONS LEADER
Captains England to semi-finals at Euro '96, where they lose on penalties to Germany
1997

MAY
GUNNER GLORY
Beats Man. United to the league title and Newcastle in the FA Cup Final to win the double
1998

JUNE
PENALTY HELL
Plays in his first World Cup but crashes out to Argentina on penalties
1999

MAY
ROYAL RECOGNITION
Receives MBE in Queen's honours list, recognising his fine service to football
2000

MAY
FA CUP MISERY
Leads Arsenal to the FA Cup Final but loses out 2-1 to rivals Liverpool
2001

1988

MAY LOSING AT WEMBLEY

Just two months after Tony Adams was made captain by George Graham, he led Arsenal out at Wembley for the Littlewoods Cup Final. The Gunners were favourites to lift the League Cup, but when they were 2-1 up, Nigel Winterburn missed a penalty and Luton came back to win 3-2 thanks to a late goal in injury time.

"We lost to Luton in the dying seconds. We had led throughout that game and I remember thinking I would be lifting the trophy."

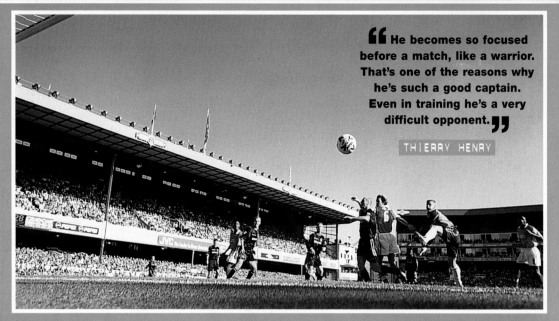

> He becomes so focused before a match, like a warrior. That's one of the reasons why he's such a good captain. Even in training he's a very difficult opponent.
>
> THIERRY HENRY

1988

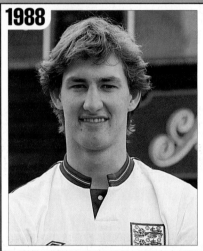

JUNE EARNING THE DONKEY TAG

After an impressive season at the heart of the Arsenal defence, Adams was selected for the England squad to play in the 1988 Euro Championships, but he had a poor game in the 3-1 defeat by Spain and the tabloid newspapers called him a 'donkey'. When the next league campaign started, fans everywhere began to taunt him, even throwing carrots at him during games.

"Well I probably get more criticism than anyone else. Since I've been at Highbury I've been called anything from a cart horse to a donkey as football supporters don't seem to rate me. But my worst critics are the Press, who take great delight in having a real go at me every time I make a slight mistake. But whenever I picked up a paper and was being criticised, I'd just toss it to one side with a giggle then forget about it. But if my mum ever read something like that, she became very upset about people having a go at her 'little boy'."

1989

MAY LIFTING THE LEAGUE TITLE

Needing to win by two goals against Liverpool on the last day of the 1989 season, Arsenal attacked for their life. The two goalscorers, Alan Smith and Michael Thomas, took the plaudits, but it was a superb team effort – led by captain Adams in defence – which brought the title back to Highbury for the first time in 18 years.

"Lifting the League championship trophy at Anfield was the proudest moment of my life. It was 18 years since the skipper of a London side held that prized piece of silverware and for me to do it – as a born and bred Londoner – was unbelievable. To parade the trophy around Anfield, the home of the champions for so many years, was like a fairytale come true. I just couldn't believe it."

1993

APRIL WINNING ARSENAL AN FA CUP FINAL PLACE

In the 1992-93 season, having won the League Cup Final against Sheffield Wednesday at Wembley, Adams and co. met Tottenham in the semi-finals of the FA Cup, wanting revenge after being beaten by their arch-rivals at the same stage in 1991. To his delight, it was the captain who scored the goal that took The Gunners back to Wembley, where they ran out 2-1 winners – with Wednesday again the beaten finalists – for the first domestic cup double in the history of English football – a unique achievement.

"I can remember Arsenal getting beaten at York in the cup and losing the semi-final to Tottenham in 1991 – that's why it meant so much. We were given the chance to put things right and it was our turn that year. Going up those steps at Wembley is a moment that will always be with me. All those years of trying were suddenly worth it."

1994

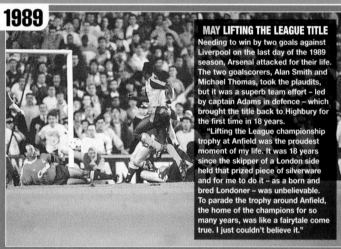

MAY FIGHTING FOR EUROPEAN GLORY

Arsenal qualified for the European Cup-Winners' Cup after their FA Cup success in 1993 and they didn't waste any time in making a big impression on the continent. Adams led Arsenal to the final of the competition, in Copenhagen, where The Gunners beat Sven Goran Eriksson's Parma side 1-0. Although the captain and his team mates didn't know it yet, 1993-94 was George Graham's last full season in charge at Highbury.

"It was unbelievable. Our fans were in every part of the stadium and the neutrals were on our side – supporting our Danish international John Jensen. Alan Smith scored a goal early in the game, we defended our lead and David Seaman was just fantastic in goal. I think it was the most satisfying trophy of my career and a really great achievement. Parma thought they only had to turn up to win the final, but we defended very well."

1994

OCTOBER LEADING OUT ENGLAND

In October 1994, seven years after making his senior debut for England, Terry Venables asked Adams to lead out his country at Wembley for the first time. England qualified for Euro '96 as hosts, so they played two years of friendly games from 1994 to 1996, and Adams made his debut as captain in the first friendly against Romania. Robert Lee scored England's goal in front of 48,000 Wembley fans in a 1-1 draw.

"It was an unbelievable feeling. To lead England out against Romania was something else! There is no higher accolade you can achieve in the game and it's something you dream about when you're a kid. I had been the captain of Arsenal since I was 21, so it helped me to cope with the big occasion. I enjoyed every minute of it and I always felt very proud to lead the side out. It's difficult to describe, but when you lead England out at Wembley it's very loud – maybe a bit like the film 'Gladiator'."

1996

JUNE CAPTAINING ENGLAND AT EURO '96

Adams remained as captain under Terry Venables at Euro '96, when football 'came home'. After a disappointing opening 1-1 draw against Switzerland, England beat the auld enemy Scotland in Group A and hammered Holland 4-1 en route to the semi-final, losing 6-5 on penalties to Germany.

"I think we were very close to winning that competition, which would have been a tremendous achievement. To out-play Germany at Wembley in the semi-final was unbelievable. I thought the performance was excellent – we played them off the park for 75 minutes, but unfortunately we just didn't get the result."

1998

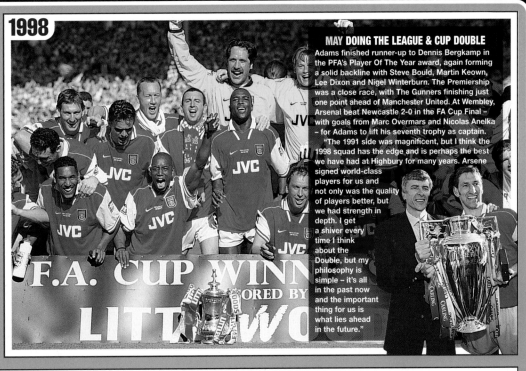

MAY DOING THE LEAGUE & CUP DOUBLE

Adams finished runner-up to Dennis Bergkamp in the PFA's Player Of The Year award, again forming a solid backline with Steve Bould, Martin Keown, Lee Dixon and Nigel Winterburn. The Premiership was a close race, with The Gunners finishing just one point ahead of Manchester United. At Wembley, Arsenal beat Newcastle 2-0 in the FA Cup Final – with goals from Marc Overmars and Nicolas Anelka – for Adams to lift his seventh trophy as captain.

"The 1991 side was magnificent, but I think the 1998 squad has the edge and is perhaps the best we have had at Highbury for many years. Arsene signed world-class players for us and not only was the quality of players better, but we had strength in depth. I get a shiver every time I think about the Double, but my philosophy is simple – it's all in the past now and the important thing for us is what lies ahead in the future."

> **" As a player and captain, his record is second to none. It's easy for me to play alongside him because he knows his job inside out. "**
>
> MARTIN KEOWN

1999

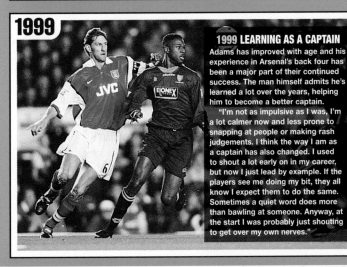

1999 LEARNING AS A CAPTAIN

Adams has improved with age and his experience in Arsenal's back four has been a major part of their continued success. The man himself admits he's learned a lot over the years, helping him to become a better captain.

"I'm not as impulsive as I was, I'm a lot calmer now and less prone to snapping at people or making rash judgements. I think the way I am as a captain has also changed. I used to shout a lot early on in my career, but now I just lead by example. If the players see me doing my bit, they all know I expect them to do the same. Sometimes a quiet word does more than bawling at someone. Anyway, at the start I was probably just shouting to get over my own nerves."

2001

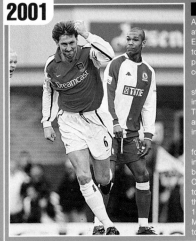

2001 LOSING THE FA CUP

Adams retired from the international game soon after Sven Goran Eriksson was named the new England coach in January 2001. With 66 caps to his name and after suffering continous injury problems in recent campaigns, he decided to concentrate on his club football with Arsenal.

His commitment to Arsenal shone through straight away, despite missing several games in 2000-01 through injury. The captain helped The Gunners to finish second in the Premiership and led Arsene Wenger's side to the last eight in the Champions League.

Some of the team's best form was reserved for the FA Cup. Adams came back from injury in time for a 3-0 home win against Blackburn before defeating arch-rivals Tottenham 2-1 at Old Trafford in the semi-finals. Arsenal travelled to the Millennium Stadium for the final and were the dominant side for most of the game, going 1-0 up through a Freddie Ljungberg goal. But Michael Owen scored two goals for Liverpool to come back to win 2-1 and lift the trophy.

HOW DID YOU SCORE?

Reckon you know everything there is to know about football? Well, now's the time to put that knowledge to the test. There's a point for each correct answer.

The blue half of Glasgow celebrate another trophy.

CROSSWORD

Use your footy knowledge to solve the crossword below!

ACROSS

8. Newcastle's former PSG defender, Alain (4)
9. Brazilian centre-back, Emerson, in Peter Reid's squad (5)
10. Sir .... Ferguson, boss set to complete a final term at Old Trafford (4)
11. Steve, Northern Ireland midfield man at Upton Park (5)
12. Hard-working Irish winger, Keith, with Middlesbrough (6)
13. Jamie, consistent Liverpool defender (9)
15. Old Trafford's promising England defender, Wes (5)
18. Skilful young striker, Francis, who made a name with The Toffees (7)
20. Bolton's Jamaican midfield star, Ricardo (7)
23. David, Villa and England goalkeeper (5)
25. Keith, winger of Man. United, Newcastle, Blackburn and Northern Ireland fame (9)
28. Boro's former Aston Villa centre-back, Ugo (6)
30. Representative used by players in salary and transfer matters (5)
32. The ...., former Southampton ground (4)
33. Defender, Spencer, who moved from Derby to Maine Road (5)
34. Paul, Aussie in England at The Riverside Stadium (4)

DOWN

1. Rivals of Stoke City, The Valiants (4, 4)
2. Leicester boss, Peter, England's former caretaker coach (6)
3. Man. United's ex-PSV star, Jaap (4)
4. Belgian striker, Cedric, brought to England by Gordon Strachan (7)
5. West Ham youngster, Jermain, loaned to Bournemouth last term (5)
6. White Hart ...., home of Tottenham Hotspur (4)
7. Norwich City's dominant club colour (6)
14. Nickname of Scotland's Ibrox giants (4)
16. Colour sported by Wrexham and Wales (3)
17. Michael, 22-year-old Everton defender (4)
19. Marc-Vivien, ex-West Ham Cameroon midfielder now with Lyon (3)
21. Sven Goran, Swede appointed as England's coach (8)
22. West Ham's extravagant Italian hitman, Paolo (7)
24. ...... Cole, Arsenal's promising young England full-back (6)
26. Celtic's big-money striker, Chris, recruited from Chelsea (6)
27. Leicester's one-time Vale winger, Steve (5)
29. Sheffield Wednesday's club nickname (4)
31. Alternative name of Mick McCarthy's Republic of Ireland side (4)

---

fourth XI

They're arguably the most successful club in Scotland, but how much do you know about Glasgow Rangers?

1 One of Rangers' many trophy successes was the European Cup-Winner's Cup in 1972. Which Russian side did they beat in the final?

2 True or false? Graeme Souness was manager between 1986 and 1991.

3 Rangers won the league on the last day of the 1990-91 season against Aberdeen. Which formidable English striker scored a brace to snatch the championship?

4 The Ibrox giants played out a European Cup 'Battle Of Britain' in 1992. Which English team did they beat both home and away?

5 Which recently retired striker is Rangers' most capped player after earning 60 caps for Scotland?

6 Paul Gascoigne joined the club for £4.3 million in July 1995. Which three clubs did he play for before this?

7 In which year did Rangers complete their run of nine consecutive league titles?

8 Dick Advocaat took over as Rangers manager in 1998. Who did he replace and which club did the Dutchman leave to take charge at Ibrox?

9 The Gers won a domestic treble in Advocaat's first term. Who did they beat in the Scottish FA Cup and League Cup finals?

10 Crowd favourite Jorg Albertz finished as the club's leading league scorer in 1999-2000. How many goals did he score?

11 Tore Andre Flo joined Rangers in November 2000. How much did the club pay for the Norwegian and which club did he sign from?

SAY WHAT?

Which of his players is Arsene Wenger talking about here?

He didn't want to travel by train. Perhaps trains are too fast for him as well.

1 POINT FOR CORRECT ANSWER

REF OFF!

Can you identify this top referee?

WHO WON IT?

The 1979 FA Cup

1 POINT FOR CORRECT ANSWER

---

connections...

Which Premiership boss connects Bryan Robson with Coventry manager Gordon Strachan?

NAME THE CLUB!

Whose recent league record is this?

	Div Two	Division One		Premiership
1			2nd	
5	6th			
10		13th		17th
15				
20	21st			20th
	'96	'97 '98 '99		'00 '01

POSITION / **SEASON**

CIVVY STREET

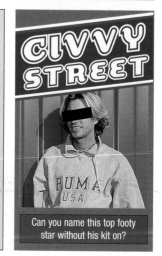

Can you name this top footy star without his kit on?

PAUL MERSON
Aston Villa

DER

BY DAYS

MATCH looks at the biggest derby games in Britain, finds out which teams have the upper hand and asks the players for their view.

DERBY DAYS ARE – WITHOUT DOUBT – THE MOST PASSIONATE GAMES IN THE FOOTBALL CALENDAR.
They're the first fixtures to look for at the start of the new season and both sets of fans wait with baited breath until the big day arrives. With local media increasing the hype, these matches traditionally draw the biggest crowds of the season and the atmosphere is electric, with fans roaring their team on from the first crunching tackle to the final whistle. Local pride is at stake and nobody wants to go into school or work after a defeat to face their so-called 'friends' who follow the opposition.

There's also tension on the pitch – the players know how important derbies are to the fans and are desperate to get one over their old rivals. But while there are many derby days during the season, some are much bigger than others – due to the stature of the clubs, the history between them and the massive support they both receive. MATCH selects the top five derbies in Britain today, finding out who's won the most games, the history of previous encounters and what the players think of these fascinating battles!

NORTH EAST DERBY

THE TEAMS

CLUB: Newcastle United
DIVISION: FA Premiership
GROUND: St James' Park
CAPACITY: 52,167
MANAGER: Bobby Robson

CLUB: Sunderland
DIVISION: FA Premiership
GROUND: Stadium Of Light
CAPACITY: 48,300
MANAGER: Peter Reid

THE GROUNDS

St James' Park

Stadium Of Light

Newcastle
Sunderland

STATS

● **FIRST DERBY PLAYED: Sunderland 2 Newcastle 3** December 24, 1899

● **HIGHEST DERBY SCORELINE: Newcastle 1 Sunderland 9** December 5, 1908

● **BIGGEST DERBY WIN: Newcastle 1 Sunderland 9** December 5, 1908

● **2000-01 (ST JAMES' PARK): Newcastle 1 Sunderland 2** November 18, 2000

● **2000-01 (STADIUM OF LIGHT): Sunderland 1 Newcastle 1** April 21, 2001

RECORDS

	P	W	D	L	F	A
● Newcastle United	124	42	39	42	183	190
● Sunderland	124	42	39	42	190	183

HISTORY: The first league meeting between the sides from Tyne and Wear took place in 1899, when Newcastle won 3-2 at Sunderland.

HOW MUCH IS AT STAKE? The two teams are situated extremely close to each other, making this a fiercely contested derby. There's the famous story about Lee Clark – an ex-Newcastle player who was sold to Sunderland – which sums up the intense rivalry. On the day of his transfer, his Newcastle-supporting father-in-law locked him out of the house and refused to speak to him. Then, after opting to wear a pro-Newcastle, anti-Sunderland T-shirt at a Newcastle game, he was placed on the transfer list by Black Cats' boss Peter Reid.

WHO'S GOT THE UPPER HAND? Surprisingly, it's honours even between the North East sides, but neither will admit the other side's as good as them! Sunderland have done well since their return to the Premiership and one of their most famous victories over Newcastle came in August 1999 when they beat Ruud Gullit's side at St James' Park, with Alan Shearer left to watch from the bench.

DID YOU KNOW? In 1909, Newcastle won their third title in five years, but that season Sunderland hammered them 9-1 at St James' Park!

WHAT DO THE PLAYERS SAY? DON HUTCHISON: "I've been quite fortunate to play in a Merseyside derby, a London derby and a North East derby – but they are all different. The North East one is definitely the most tense. In the Merseyside derby, they are all quite friendly because a lot of fans come from the same family, but the North East derbies have an atmosphere of their own. Up there, you're either red and white or black and white, and there is a hatred. Every pro enjoys derby matches and it's the greatest feeling in the world to go away to your rivals and get a win in front of their fans."

MANCHESTER DERBY

THE TEAMS

CLUB: Manchester United
DIVISION: FA Premiership
GROUND: Old Trafford
CAPACITY: 68,936
MANAGER: Sir Alex Ferguson

CLUB: Manchester City
DIVISION: Division One
GROUND: Maine Road
CAPACITY: 34,026
MANAGER: Kevin Keegan

THE GROUNDS

Old Trafford

Maine Road

Manchester

STATS

- **FIRST DERBY PLAYED: Man. United 5 Man. City 1** October 3, 1891
- **HIGHEST DERBY SCORELINE: Man. City 3 Man. United 4** May 5, 1971
- **BIGGEST DERBY WIN: Man. United 6 Man. City 1** January 23, 1926
- **2000-01 (MAINE ROAD): Man. City 0 Man. United 1** November 18, 2000
- **2000-01 (OLD TRAFFORD): Man. United 1 Man. City 1** April 21, 2001

RECORDS

	P	W	D	L	F	A
● Manchester City	137	36	46	55	182	200
● Manchester United	137	55	46	36	200	182

HISTORY: The first competitive Manchester derby took place in 1891, an FA Cup First Round Qualifier which United won 5-1. It was three years before the sides met in a league game and United again won comfortably, this time 5-2. The derby continued through relegation and promotion for both sides, as well as surviving two world wars – in WW2 United even had to ground-share with City when Old Trafford was damaged by bombing!

HOW MUCH IS AT STAKE? City fans have a distinct hatred of Manchester United – their more successful neighbours – who have the better of them in derbies stretching back 110 years. They would love to bring The Red Devils back down to earth with a bang, but United have dominated these fixtures in recent years and will want to continue their proud record.

WHO'S GOT THE UPPER HAND? After a four-year break following City's experience into the lower divisions, the Manchester derby resumed in 2000-01 – to everyone's delight – but only for one season. In two hard-fought matches, a David Beckham free-kick stole a 1-0 win at Maine Road, while the two sides drew at Old Trafford.

DID YOU KNOW? Sir Matt Busby, Manchester United's legendary manager from 1945 to 1969, used to play for Manchester City in his playing days!

WHAT DO THE PLAYERS SAY? DENIS IRWIN: "It's special for the city of Manchester, I think. The city has got two massive clubs, which are both very well supported. The rivalry between both of the clubs is brilliant. You cannot beat derby days, you can go anywhere for a derby but this is the best one in the country. Obviously it's the only derby I've played in, but it takes a lot of beating."

GARY NEVILLE: "It is something that everyone missed in Manchester and it stirs everybody up. There is a lot of passion involved and our fans have a bit of fun when we play each other. We need this excitement in the season, like the Liverpool clubs get with their derby."

OLD FIRM DERBY

THE TEAMS

CLUB: Rangers
DIVISION: SPL
GROUND: Ibrox Stadium
CAPACITY: 50,467
MANAGER: Dick Advocaat

CLUB: Celtic
DIVISION: SPL
GROUND: Celtic Park
CAPACITY: 60,506
MANAGER: Martin O'Neill

THE GROUNDS

Ibrox

Celtic Park

Glasgow

STATS

- **FIRST DERBY PLAYED: Celtic 2 Rangers 5** May 1888
- **HIGHEST DERBY SCORELINE: Rangers 8 Celtic 1** January 1, 1943
- **BIGGEST DERBY WIN: Rangers 8 Celtic 1** January 1, 1943
- **2000-01 (IBROX): Rangers 5 Celtic 1** Nov. 26, 2000 **Rangers 0 Celtic 3** Apr. 29, 2001
- **2000-01 (CELTIC): Celtic 6 Rangers 2** Aug. 27, 2000 **Celtic 1 Rangers 0** Feb. 11, 2001
- **2000-01 (LEAGUE CUP): Celtic 3 Rangers 1** February 7, 2001

RECORDS

	P	W	D	L	F	A
● Rangers	337	133	86	118	491	452
● Celtic	337	118	86	133	452	491

HISTORY: Celtic were formed in 1887 and a year later the first Old Firm derby took place, with Celtic beating Rangers 5-2 at Parkhead. The teams have met many times since then, due to the nature of the league where each team plays each other four times. The teams have also faced each other in 24 cup finals over the years.

HOW MUCH IS AT STAKE? There is a massive rivalry between the two sides and is it probably the most tense derby in Britain; those who have played in it say it's the biggest club match in the world. As well as being close neighbours in Glasgow, there is an off-the-field rivalry due to the different religious denominations that each side represents – Rangers supporters are traditionally Protestants while Celtic fans are Catholics. The pair are also the two strongest teams in Scottish football, which has added an extra competitive edge to the derby.

WHO'S GOT THE UPPER HAND? Although Rangers can claim to be the most successful team in Scottish history, Celtic won the treble in 2000-01 with Rangers managing just one Old Firm derby victory in their five meetings. Martin O'Neill had earlier endeared himself to the Celtic fans with a 6-2 home victory in his first ever derby.

DID YOU KNOW? In October 1971, it was announced over the tannoy – during a match at Ibrox – that nearby Partick were beating Celtic 4-0 in the League Cup Final. Hearing this, Rangers fans left the game early to travel to Hampden Park to jeer the Celtic fans!

WHAT DO THE PLAYERS SAY? JONATHAN GOULD: "Wherever you go in Scotland, people say the Old Firm game is the best derby in the world. The feelings shown by the fans are deeper than just football, it's to do with religion and tradition too. The football is very passionate up here and from what I've seen, the atmosphere at an Old Firm game is twice as good as that of an English derby. There's a great deal of pressure from Celtic supporters to win every derby game you play in."

MERSEYSIDE DERBY

THE TEAMS

CLUB: Liverpool
DIVISION: FA Premiership
GROUND: Anfield
CAPACITY: 45,362
MANAGER: Gerard Houllier

CLUB: Everton
DIVISION: FA Premiership
GROUND: Goodison Park
CAPACITY: 40,260
MANAGER: Walter Smith

THE GROUNDS

Anfield

Goodison Park

Liverpool

STATS

- **FIRST DERBY PLAYED:** Everton 3 Liverpool 0 October 1894
- **HIGHEST DERBY SCORELINE:** Liverpool 7 Everton 4 February 11, 1933
- **BIGGEST DERBY WIN:** Everton 0 Liverpool 5 November 6, 1982
- **2000-01 (ANFIELD):** Liverpool 3 Everton 1 October 29, 2000
- **2000-01 (GOODISON):** Everton 2 Liverpool 3 April 16, 2001

RECORDS

	P	W	D	L	F	A
Liverpool	188	70	57	61	255	225
Everton	188	61	57	70	225	255

HISTORY: Everton used to play at Anfield, but following an argument with the ground's owner, John Houlding, they left and Houlding set up his own team – Liverpool. This started a great rivalry. When the two sides first met in a league game, in October 1894, 44,000 fans packed into Goodison Park to see Everton win 3-0. Two of the most memorable games of recent years – although not for Toffees' fans – were the 1986 FA Cup Final, in which Liverpool won a replay 1-0 to seal the Double, and the 1989 FA Cup Final, which Liverpool won 3-2.

HOW MUCH IS AT STAKE? There's plenty of history and passion with this fixture, but this is one of the friendlier derbies – at least off the field, as families divide into red and blue. But on the pitch it's a different story as the two sides battle away for the pride of Merseyside. Even the normally laid-back Sander Westerveld had a fight with Everton striker Francis Jeffers two seasons ago!

WHO'S GOT THE UPPER HAND? The record tells a tale of equality, but Everton fell foul of Liverpool's dominance of the domestic game in the '80s, losing several derbies. In recent years, there have been several incidents to keep the fans entertained and last season, 2000-01, Liverpool did the league double over their neighbours.

DID YOU KNOW? Everton won the First Division title in 1984-85, but Liverpool got their own back a year later by winning the Division One championship two points ahead of their Merseyside neighbours.

WHAT DO THE PLAYERS SAY? ROBBIE FOWLER: "A lot of the players have grown up around Liverpool and we know what the derby is all about. Families are divided on the day and maybe for weeks afterwards, depending on how the result goes. It's a really funny game around the city of Liverpool – it can really divide families. You can have brothers and sisters who are Evertonians and mums and dads who are Liverpudlians. I don't think that happens anywhere else in the world – it's very unusual."

NORTH LONDON DERBY

THE TEAMS

CLUB: Arsenal
DIVISION: FA Premiership
GROUND: Highbury
CAPACITY: 38,500
MANAGER: Arsene Wenger

CLUB: Tottenham Hotspur
DIVISION: FA Premiership
GROUND: White Hart Lane
CAPACITY: 36,236
MANAGER: Glenn Hoddle

THE GROUNDS

Highbury

White Hart Lane

London

STATS

- **FIRST DERBY PLAYED:** Tottenham 2 Arsenal 1 November 19, 1887
- **HIGHEST DERBY SCORELINE:** Tottenham 4 Arsenal 4 1958, 1962 & 1963
- **BIGGEST DERBY WIN:** Tottenham 0 Arsenal 6 March 6, 1935
- **2000-01 (WHITE HART LANE):** Tottenham 1 Arsenal 1 December 18, 2000
- **2000-01 (HIGHBURY):** Arsenal 2 Tottenham 0 March 31, 2001
- **2000-01 (FA CUP):** Arsenal 2 Tottenham 1 April 8, 2001

RECORDS

	P	W	D	L	F	A
ARSENAL	141	58	34	49	201	185
TOTTENHAM	141	49	34	58	185	201

HISTORY: The first North London derby took place on November 19, 1887 on The Marshes – Tottenham's old playing ground. Tottenham were leading 2-1 when the game was abandoned 15 minutes from time. Arsenal had turned up late and the darkness brought the game to an end – there were no floodlights in those days!

HOW MUCH IS AT STAKE? Well it's not the fiercest of derbies, but there's no love lost between both sets of supporters, so the rivalry is probably stronger in the stands than on the pitch, with many of the players not understanding what the game means to the supporters. Ex-Gooner Paul Merson was one player who was very aware of the rivalry – he refused a move to Spurs from Middlesbrough because of his Arsenal connections. But George Graham did swap colours and came in for a lot of stick from Tottenham fans during his spell in charge of the club after his previous tenure as Arsenal manager.

WHO'S GOT THE UPPER HAND? Arsenal have won nine more games than their arch-rivals and love to sing their chorus of '1-0 to the Arsenal' as often as possible! A high percentage of the games have ended in draws, which is quite typical of derby games, and neither side has managed to score a large number of goals.

DID YOU KNOW? Arsenal actually persuaded Spurs to move to White Hart Lane! When the two sides met in 1899, Tottenham's Northumberland Park ground could barely hold the 14,000 fans who turned up for the game, so Spurs decided to look for a new ground, which was built on the site of White Hart Lane.

WHAT DO THE PLAYERS SAY? ASHLEY COLE: "I think everyone is up for the derby games a bit more and all of us look forward to them coming around. It's a good experience and obviously I'd like to play in a few more."
TIM SHERWOOD: "There is pressure on the Spurs players to do well, but it's more important to emulate Arsenal's achievements than to beat them in one-off games."

ROUTE ONE EXTRA!

DID YOU KNOW?
Italian footballers have given Michael Owen the top nickname 'Piccoletto', which roughly translates into English as 'Little Man'.

CAN YOU SEE YOURSELF

John Hartson
Coventry City

...playing another position?
"Maybe centre-back – if you look at Dion Dublin, he made the transition from the centre of defence. If you're big, strong and can head the ball, then you can probably play at the back. It's just getting to know some positional sense, that's the only position for me if I changed."

...taking a training session?
"Yeah, definitely. It's something I want to get into, I'd like to stay in the game when I finish and I'm hoping to take my badges. I've worked with a lot of top managers and in a few years' time, when I'm close to the end of the my career, it's something I'd think about. I've done some training for kids and I've taken the warm-ups and warm-downs with the lads."

...answering back to the gaffer?
"Yeah, definitely – as long as it's constructive. I think you need to have your say because you're cheating yourself and the manager if you just agree with what he says. I think if he's a good manager, a great manager, he'll listen to what the players have to say."

...decking a referee?
"No, definitely not. I've been tempted a few times, but that's something I couldn't do. That's all 'banned for life' stuff and if I got banned I don't know what I'd do on Saturday afternoons!"

...going into football journalism?
"TV or radio possibly, 'cos I do a lot of TV work now for Wales – I can speak fluent Welsh. I think there's only me and Ewan Roberts that can speak it, so I think there's a chance I could commentate on a few games. I don't think I could ever criticise a player – not without being able to justify it. But none of the ex-players would do that anyway."

...playing non-league footy?
"I don't think so. I've been fortunate really that I've made good money through the game. If I can invest that, I shouldn't have to go down that route. Hopefully when I finish I'll have enough to just call it a day."

PLAYERS LOVE CHARIDEEE!

Andy Cole visited Zimbabwe to see underprivileged kids.

Okay, hands up if you harp on about how much money footballers get and how greedy they all are. Well, it's time to eat humble pie, because two of the biggest stars in the Premiership have started up their own charities to help those less fortunate than themselves. Manchester United striker Andy Cole went over to Zimbabwe a couple of years ago to see the plight of the orphaned African children and he was so upset by what he saw that he lent his name to a charity to help them out. **"Going to Zimbabwe made me stop and think about how much I have,"** said Cole. **"I decided I had to do something to help these children."** The England man holds regular gala evenings, on behalf of the Andy Cole Children's Foundation, which his team-mates regularly attend, helping to raise £50,000 a time. The money goes towards farming projects and providing much needed homes for orphaned children. Top man, eh?

Meanwhile, Arsenal forward Kanu is also raising money for a project very close to his heart. Geddit? Yes, the Kanu Heart Foundation was set up to bring children with heart problems from Kanu's homeland, Nigeria, to England for treatment. Kanu's top fundraising efforts are helped by his team mates Thierry Henry and Patrick Vieira, who are both patrons of the charity. **"The people we are trying to help are a lot less fortunate than some and they cannot afford to have the operations they need,"** explained Kanu. **"There are about 200 children in Nigeria waiting to see if we can help them. Whenever you see the children you have pity for them."**

Kanu helps children with heart problems.

Cole shows off his skills to the kids.

Kanu helped save these kids' lives.

BARKING!
FIFA'S NEW CHIEF EXECUTIVE WAS AN EXCITABLE CHAP!

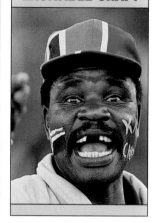

> I can imagine the game was poor to watch but we showed a lot of fight and everyone who was on the pitch at least wanted to play for Newcastle United.

Alan Shearer describes a Newcastle match. And the somewhat traitorous opposition players!

THE PRESSURE OF YOUTH!

Anyone who remembers Paul Gascoigne's rise to fame, and his subsequent fall from grace, will understand the pressure being put on Joe Cole. The young West Ham star is already well known as the next great thing. For many young players, it would be too much to bear, but Joe has taken it all in his stride and, as he told Route 1, he just doesn't believe the hype! **"I'm not really burdened by other peoples' expectations at all,"** he shrugged. **"I learned at an early age that high expectations can only lead to disappointment. Others before me have been compared to players of the past, and people tend to draw similarities between me and Paul Gascoigne. While I can see the reason behind that, I'm my own player and I will fulfil my own potential with time. The only pressure comes from myself. I'm still trying to get into the international set-up – if I was to believe all the hype I'd have captained England by now!"** Now there's a thought.

MERSE'S VILLA NON-THRILLA!

Life is hard being an Aston Villa fan. It seems that the players and supporters are suffering a severe case of inferiority complex as the club battles to keep up with the Premiership big boys. And, as Paul Merson revealed, every year they're faced with the same prospect of plenty of graft but limited success. **"It's hard for the Villa fans and the players,"** admitted Merson, himself a big hit with the supporters. **"The squad goes on summer holiday, comes back, trains hard and then it's into the season. And when you start the season, in how many other sports can you say you know you can't win the prize at the end? That's the reality. You don't just make up 30 points on Manchester United overnight. We were 30 points behind them at the end of last season and the season before last."** And probably this season and the next. It could be worse Merse, you could be playing for Birmingham City!

MATCH ENTERTAINERS

MATT JANSEN
Blackburn Rovers

CAPTAIN Marvels

ALAN SHEARER

> " He is outstanding captaincy material. He can be trusted to go out, give his best and set an example to the rest. "
>
> KEVIN KEEGAN

ALAN SHEARER TIMELINE...

APRIL
DEBUT DAY
Makes his first start for Southampton, scoring a hat-trick in a 4-2 win over Arsenal

1988

OCTOBER
CUP START
Nets the first cup goals of his career in the 2-0 League Cup win against York

1989

JUNE
EURO WINNER
Scores the winner for England's Under-21s in the final of the Toulon tournament

1990

FEBRUARY
ENGLAND CAP
Earns his first cap for England under Graham Taylor and nets against France

MAY
TOP SCORER
Ends the season as top scorer for The Saints on 13 goals

1991

JUNE
BIG-MONEY MOVE
Joins Blackburn in an exchange deal worth an estimated £3.3 million

1992

AUGUST
DEBUT STUNNER
Nets a brace on his debut for Blackburn in the 3-3 draw at Crystal Palace

DECEMBER
INJURY HELL
Sustains cruciate ligament damage on Boxing Day and is ruled out for season

1993

SEPTEMBER
COMEBACK KID
Scores on his comeback in 1-1 draw with Sheff. Wed.

MARCH
SHEARER'S CENTURY
Scores his 100th league goal in win over Chelsea

1994

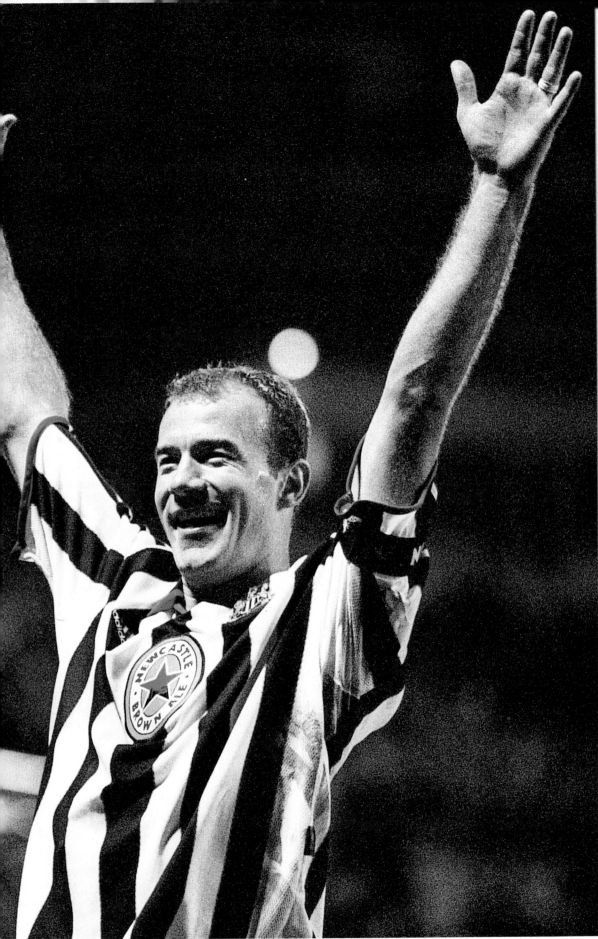

WHEN ALAN SHEARER CAME home to Tyneside in July 1996 for a record-breaking £15 million, thousands of Newcastle fans came to welcome the local boy done good. It was a dream come true for Shearer and nine months later he realised another ambition when he was appointed captain of The Magpies; he had already taken the England armband after Glenn Hoddle assumed control of the national side after Euro '96.

His mix of power, aggression and proven goalscoring ability has made him an icon with the fans and an inspirational captain among his team mates at club and international level. It's surely a crying shame that Shearer has never led any of his sides to any trophies, despite reaching two successive FA Cup Finals with Newcastle. But after retiring from England, the Magpies skipper is hoping to put his injuries behind him as he makes a determined effort to lead Newcastle to glory.

MATCH looks back at the key moments in Shearer's career as Newcastle and England captain.

ALAN SHEARER FACTFILE

BORN: August 13, 1970 in Newcastle

NATIONALITY: English

POSITION: Striker

HEIGHT: 6ft 0ins

WEIGHT: 12st 6lbs

FORMER CLUBS: Southampton, Blackburn Rovers

SIGNED: From Blackburn Rovers for £15 million on July 30, 1996

NEWCASTLE DEBUT: v Everton on August 17, 1996

APPOINTED CAPTAIN: March 1997 (Newcastle) & September 1996 (England)

TOTAL NEWCASTLE GAMES/GOALS: 175/93

TROPHIES WON AS CAPTAIN: None

INTERNATIONAL HONOURS: England 63/30, England B, Under-21 & Youth

---

MAY
ROVER THE MOON
Wins the Premier League with Blackburn on the last day of the campaign and named Player Of The Year

MAY
GOLDEN MAN
Wins the Premiership Golden Boot after five league hat-tricks

1995

JUNE
BREAKING THE DUCK
Ends goal drought in the opening match of Euro '96

JULY
RECORD TRANSFER
Moves to Newcastle for a world record £15 million

1996

MARCH
TOP TOON HONOUR
Leads out Newcastle for the first time as captain

APRIL
AWARD WINNER
Wins Player Of The Year award for second time

1997

MAY
CUP FINAL UPSET
Loses the FA Cup Final to Arsenal

JUNE
PENALTY HELL
Loses on penalties to Argentina in epic World Cup tie

1998

NOVEMBER
EURO JOY
Plays in Euro 2000 play-off victory over Scotland

MAY
WEMBLEY DEFEAT
Loses the FA Cup Final for the second year in a row, to Man. United

1999

JUNE
EURO TRASH
Scores to beat Germany but England bow out

2000

APRIL
INJURY SETBACK
Undergoes an operation on his knee injury in Colorado

SEPTEMBER
RECORD BREAKER
Becomes the first player to score 200 goals in the Premiership

2001

1996

> **"** Alan's a terrific player, he's a great leader and a good personality. **"**
>
> BOBBY ROBSON

SEPTEMBER BECOMING ENGLAND CAPTAIN

After a scoring drought at international level, Shearer silenced his critics in the Press by winning the Golden Boot award at Euro '96. When Glenn Hoddle took charge of the national side soon after the tournament he offered the striker the captain's armband. Shearer was handed a probation period of three games, but as usual he confirmed his promise at the earliest opportunity – in his first game as skipper – when he scored England's third goal in the crucial 3-0 World Cup Qualifier win in Moldova.

"Being named captain of England was one of the best things to ever happen to me in my career. I've won a few honours – both individually and with Blackburn, and playing for Newcastle is even better than I expected it to be, but captaining England has to go down as my proudest moment in the game. I don't think there's much that can beat leading out your country. Whatever happens to me now in my life, no-one can ever take that away from me."

1997

MARCH LEADING OUT NEWCASTLE UNITED

Shearer was a huge hero on Tyneside following his £15 million transfer from Blackburn Rovers – even before he'd kicked a ball. He didn't disappoint on the field though – sharing 49 goals in 1996-97 with Les Ferdinand after the two England striker formed a superb partnership in attack. Shearer fulfilled a life-long ambition when he was made captain of the side by Kenny Dalglish in March 1997 following Kevin Keegan's surprise resignation from the club.

"Being named captain was great. Being skipper of my hometown club – the team I had always supported – is a great honour. I always said that I must have been doing something right to even be considered for the job of captaining Newcastle! I'm proud to wear the armband and I accept all of the responsibility that comes with the job."

1997

AUGUST SUFFERING A SERIOUS INJURY

The striker had a brilliant summer in 1997, becoming the first England captain to lift a trophy on foreign soil by winning Le Tournoi. But disaster struck when, in a pre-season club tournament in July, Shearer caught his foot in the turf, fracturing his fibula and rupturing ligaments. He was out of action for seven months.

"It was the second serious injury of my career, but they're all serious when surgery is required. You have to be positive – there are other people who are a lot worse off than you and that's what I kept telling myself during the injury. But it's not easy, I won't pretend it is. When you've been denied the only thing you've been used to since you left school, it's pretty hard to take. There are times when you think there's no light at the end of the tunnel, but you just have to get on with your life. There was a huge incentive for me to get back quickly, playing for Newcastle and obviously with England in the 1998 World Cup."

1998

> **"** Shearer's a legend in Newcastle. He's my role model, I look up to him and he's a fantastic player **"**
>
> SHOLA AMEOBI

MAY LOSING THE FA CUP

Shearer came back earlier than expected from serious injury to score some important goals for Newcastle, including the winner against Sheffield United in the semi-final of the FA Cup which took the Magpies to Wembley. But Arsenal, already Premier League champions, were too strong on the day and beat Shearer's Newcastle 2-0.

"It was very disappointing for us. You never like losing, let alone at Wembley, but it wasn't our day. People said Newcastle's name was on the cup, but it just doesn't work out that way. I used to say things like that but I learned to shut up a few years ago because a lot of the time it didn't happen. The truth is, you can never really tell what is going to happen."

1999

AUGUST COMMITTING HIS FUTURE TO NEWCASTLE

In August 1999, Shearer appeared in front of a packed press conference to announce that he had signed a new five-year deal. He had joined the club just three years previously – but the new deal would effectively keep him at Newcastle for the rest of his career; it also included a coaching option.

"It was always a big move for me. I certainly intended seeing out my five years, which I've obviously done, and I signed an extension to my contract because playing for Newcastle United has been everything, and more, that I wanted it to be. The only thing that's missing now – I say the only thing, it's a big thing – is actually trophies, but hopefully that isn't too far away. I've got years left though and I would be very surprised if I was to go anywhere else to play now."

1999

AUGUST WATCHING FROM THE BENCH

The 1999-2000 season started badly for the Newcastle captain when he was sent-off in the opening-day defeat by Aston Villa. Two defeats and a draw later, Shearer was dropped for the vital derby clash against Sunderland at St James' Park. There had been reports that he didn't get on with then Newcastle manager Ruud Gullit and a 2-1 defeat merely intensified matters.

"I'd never been dropped in my career before that match, so to find myself on the bench for such an important game was a big shock to me. When I spoke to Ruud Gullit he told me I wasn't worthy of a place in the side. I didn't agree, but I went on the bench and didn't moan. I've always got on with my football, no matter what, so I wasn't going to complain. The manager obviously had his reasons for dropping me and it was his job to select the team he thought had the best chance of winning the match in hand. On the night, the team didn't win."

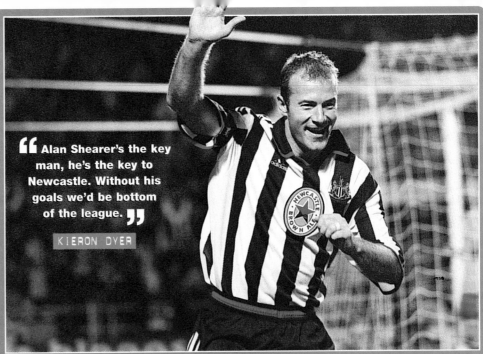

> **Alan Shearer's the key man, he's the key to Newcastle. Without his goals we'd be bottom of the league.**
> KIERON DYER

2000

> **There is something special about leading your country and it should fall to special players. Alan is in that category.**
> GLENN HODDLE

JUNE BEATING GERMANY

Shearer was determined to lead his country to Euro 2000 success under the tutelage of his former idol and club manager Kevin Keegan. It started badly though, with England losing their opening match to Portugal 3-2. In the second game of the Finals Shearer headed home David Beckham's cross to secure England's first tournament win over Germany for 34 years. It was just what the fans back home wanted.

"You could see the elation on my face when I scored, but it was nothing compared to what I felt at the final whistle. I was minus four years old when we last beat Germany in 1966! We were tough to beat. I thought our 'keeper and back four were fantastic and it was a very special victory for us. It was a long time coming – it's just a shame it wasn't the final."

2000

JUNE BOWING OUT AT EURO 2000

After one defeat and one victory, England had to draw, at least, against Romania in their last group game of Euro 2000. But at 2-2, with just seconds remaining, Phil Neville conceded a penalty. Romania converted the spot-kick and Shearer and co. caught an early plane home.

"We know we could have done much better and that's what hurt us the most. We had a good bunch of players – it's just we didn't play well. The players have to take the responsibility now, we're the ones who had to show we were good enough and we didn't do that. We made some mistakes and we should have done better with certain things that happened in the game."

2000

JULY SAYING GOODBYE

Shearer announced before leaving for Euro 2000 that he would retire from international football after the tournament was over – no matter how well England performed. The striker decided that with all his past injuries it would be far better to concentrate on playing club football, which would give him a break in the summer. The national captain unfortunately bowed out on a low, but he can be proud of his excellent goalscoring ratio of 30 goals from 63 games.

"You don't let the honour of captaining your country go lightly. Being England captain has been the greatest part of my football career to date. It was a very tough decision for me to make, but I want to see more of my family and I want to stay at my best. To do that I'll need to have some rest and, now that I won't have to play football in the summer, I can do that. I've had serious injuries and if I don't rest now they could take their toll."

2001-02

DECEMBER SEARCHING FOR SUCCESS

Without a trophy in his five-year spell at St James' Park, Shearer still has a burning desire to lead his hometown club to success and, as captain, win a trophy for the fans of the Toon Army – so can The Magpies do it?

"There wouldn't be anything better for me now, I don't think you'd be able to top that. It's been a case of, so near but yet so far since I've been at Newcastle. We've finished second in the league, we've been to two cup finals, we've been in the Champions League – but we haven't been able to clear that final hurdle. Maybe in the future – this year, next year, the year after that – it might be our turn? We certainly hope so and it won't be for want of trying."

HOW DID YOU SCORE?
This is your last chance to rack up some points to see how good your football knowledge really is. Remember to fill in your answers in the boxes on page 106.

THE MEGA WORD SPOT

Can you spot the skilful samba stars of South American football hiding in the grid below?

O	Z	J	V	E	J	A	R	D	E	L	J	P	O	C	L	S	M	T
C	O	B	O	O	Q	N	T	A	M	Q	V	B	O	E	Y	N	A	U
V	A	H	B	A	T	I	S	T	U	T	A	A	S	S	D	O	R	A
Y	A	F	N	R	O	N	A	L	D	O	Z	S	O	A	I	S	Q	L
Z	G	M	U	I	D	C	Z	H	O	L	E	S	R	R	D	R	U	M
A	O	H	P	F	G	U	A	R	Y	N	P	E	O	L	A	E	E	E
L	N	L	I	E	R	R	O	R	N	D	O	D	M	E	A	M	S	I
A	Z	W	R	C	T	M	E	L	L	W	L	A	A	G	T	E	K	D
Y	A	D	A	Q	A	A	E	S	H	O	B	S	C	N	S	W	O	A
A	L	L	G	R	O	D	E	I	V	O	S	P	O	A	I	Q	D	Z
Q	E	U	I	C	C	R	F	L	A	H	D	E	N	I	L	S	O	N
D	S	O	C	H	I	L	A	V	E	R	T	M	C	C	U	O	I	A
B	G	K	Y	T	L	F	C	T	C	N	J	R	E	R	A	R	A	Z
J	Y	O	D	R	A	L	L	A	G	S	U	D	I	E	P	T	N	O
H	F	W	B	Q	A	G	N	U	D	I	N	P	C	S	T	E	U	T
I	L	A	L	F	P	O	D	L	A	V	I	R	A	P	L	G	C	E
Z	R	Q	W	C	O	R	D	O	B	A	N	F	O	O	I	A	A	B
O	B	S	E	R	N	A	S	F	K	G	H	B	G	W	C	I	A	D
U	G	Q	Y	G	D	I	Z	J	I	B	O	B	Q	V	O	X	Y	B

- ACUNA
- ALMEIDA
- AMOROSO
- ANGEL
- AYALA
- BATISTUTA
- BASSEDAS
- BETO
- CAFU
- CARLOS
- CESAR
- CHILAVERT
- CONCEICAO
- CORDOBA
- CRESPO
- DE LA CRUZ
- DENILSON
- DIDA
- DUNGA
- EMERSON
- GALLARDO
- GONZALES
- JARDEL
- JUNINHO
- LOPEZ
- MARQUES
- ORTEGA
- OVIEDO
- PAULISTA
- RIVALDO
- ROMARIO
- RONALDO
- SERGINHO
- SERNA
- VAMPETA

MATCHfacts CODE BREAKER
CAN YOU SOLVE IT?

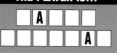

To keep his starting XI secret, a football manager has coded the name of his star player. The letters have been turned into numbers, but can you work out who this player is? He could play for any team covered by MATCHfacts.

CRACK THE CODE!

| 26 | 23 | 18 | 5 | 26 |
| 24 | 1 | 25 | 7 | 4 | 23 | 9 |

THE PLAYER IS...

| | A | | | |
| | | | | | A |

1-0
All of these games finished 1-0, but who scored the winner?

1 2000 FA Cup Final Aston Villa v Chelsea

2 Euro 2000 England v Germany

3 2000-2001 Arsenal v Man. United

4 2000 WC Qualifiers England v Germany

5 2000-2001 Man. United v West Ham

1 POINT PER CORRECT ANSWER

WHO AM I?

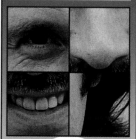

Can you guess the name of this player from these statements?

1 I was born in Rotherham back in 1963.

2 I began my career in 1982 with Leeds United.

3 I've been with my current club for 11 years.

4 I have many England caps.

2 POINTS FOR CORRECT ANSWER

How much do you really know about Leeds United's history?

fifth XI

David O'Leary has started to build a great squad for the future, but how much do you know about the club's past?

1 Leeds United have only won the FA Cup once in their history. In which year did they lift the trophy and who did they beat in the final?

2 Which famous United manager spearheaded some of the club's finest days between 1961 and 1974?

3 Which rather outspoken manager took charge of the Yorkshire giants for only 24 days in 1974?

4 Leeds pipped Manchester United to the title in 1992. Who was the captain of the side during that campaign?

5 Eric Cantona joined Leeds United in 1991. But which French club did the enigmatic star sign from and who did he later join for £1.2 million?

6 The Elland Road club last reached a Wembley final in 1996. Who beat them to the League Cup trophy that day and what was the score?

7 True or false? Leeds hold the Premiership record for the fewest number of goals scored in a season.

8 How many Premiership goals did Jimmy Floyd Hasselbaink score for Leeds before controversially moving to Atletico Madrid in 1999?

9 Which two Leeds players were sent-off in the first leg of the Champions League tie against top German side 1860 Munich in August 2000?

10 Against which team did Australian Mark Viduka score his first, long-awaited Premiership goal for Leeds?

11 Which striker scored the winning goal for David O'Leary's side in the impressive 1-0 Champions League victory over Italian giants Lazio?

WHO WON IT?

The 2000 European Cup

2 POINTS FOR CORRECT ANSWER

All Nations

Which countries do these stars play for?

1 Pavel Nedved
2 Luis Figo
3 Zlatko Zahovic
4 Raul
5 Jesper Gronkjaer

2 POINTS PER CORRECT ANSWER

LUIS FIGO
Real Madrid

MATCH
ENTERTAINERS

Presenting the top 50 players of last season, as exclusively rated by **MATCHfacts**.

THE 2000-01 PREMIERSHIP SEASON SEEMED over in weeks as bookies began to shut up shop in October, believing the title race was all but over. Man. United won the league of course, but it wasn't just Sheringham, Giggs, Keane and Becks who made an impression.

Patrick Vieira was head and shoulders above his opponents at times and Thierry Henry scored 17 goals as Arsenal finished runners-up in the Premiership. Sami Hyypia, Steven Gerrard and Michael Owen all had memorable moments as Liverpool lifted a treble of trophies. And as Leeds went one better than Man. United by making it through to the semi-finals of the Champions League, Rio Ferdinand, Lee Bowyer and Alan Smith showed a maturity beyond their years.

Other commendable performances came from members of the Ipswich and Charlton teams that surprised everyone with their success in the top flight. Sunderland, too, showed that team spirit and togetherness could go a long way, but all of these sides produced some outstanding individuals.

Other sides might have been less pleased with their progress in the 2000-01 season, but there were still plenty of players who stood out as their own club's Player Of The Year – and their form over the whole season is recognised over the next ten pages.

The winner of this year's Matchman Of The Season award has performed at the highest level throughout his long, successful career. You can find out our prestigious winner – as MATCH counts down the best 50 players of last season – by turning the page now!

MATCHMAN OF THE YEAR AWARDS

1997-1998
Dennis Bergkamp *Arsenal*
1998-1999
Tony Adams *Arsenal*
1999-2000
Paolo di Canio *West Ham*

In MATCHfacts, everyone who plays more than 15 minutes in a game is awarded a rating out of ten and the best player from each side is given a 'star rating'. Every month in MATCH, the ratings are combined to give each player an average score. The winner in every division is then presented with our prestigious Matchman Of The Month award. The monthly awards recognise a good run of form, but the seasonal awards are a true reflection of consistently outstanding performance.

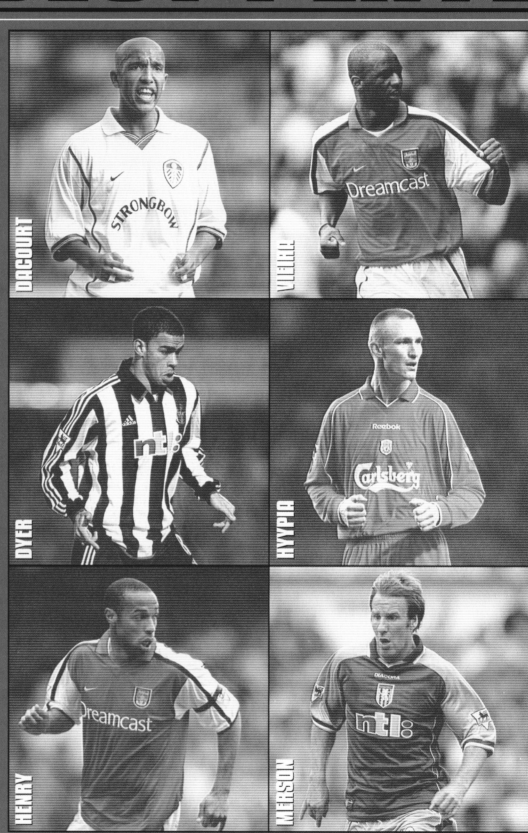

DACOURT

VIEIRA

DYER

HYYPIA

HENRY

MERSON

RS OF 2000-01!

SORENSEN

GIGGS

ZOLA

SAVAGE

COLE

SULLIVAN

BECKHAM

FERDINAND

GERRARD

1

RYAN GIGGS
Manchester United

Age: 28 **Position:** Midfield

Lowdown: While David Beckham took the early season plaudits and Teddy Sheringham walked away with the PFA Player Of The Year award, Ryan Giggs continued to weave his magic in one of his best seasons ever in a Red Devils shirt. Giggsy's wing wizardry was on show throughout the season as Man. United won their third title in a row – he scored seven goals and set up countless others with his tantalising runs and accurate crossing. The Wales star notched up nine star ratings from 27 league games – that's one MATCHfacts star man award every three games – and earned an outstanding average rating of 7.33 to narrowly beat his United team-mate Roy Keane and win the 2000-01 Matchman Of The Season award.

CONGRATULATIONS ON WINNING THE MATCHMAN OF THE SEASON AWARD FOR 2000-01!
"Thank you, I'm really pleased to have won MATCH's Player Of The Season. It was probably the most consistent season I've had and that's something I've been working hard on. It was a good season overall for the whole team, with winning the Premiership for the third season running. We expected to do better in Europe, but that's something we'll be working on this season."

WERE YOU PLEASED WITH YOUR FORM DURING THE CAMPAIGN?
"Yeah, aside from the odd injury I think I had a fairly decent season. I can play better and I'm still at the stage where I haven't arrived at my peak yet. I could score more goals and there are games where I have played a bit below-par. But when I played well, the team tended to play with me. I'm forever criticising myself, that's the way I am. I've got to the stage now where I don't actually need any critics any more because they're simply not as critical as I am."

WHAT WAS YOUR OPINION OF UNITED'S SEASON?
"Good! We always set out to win the championship and we did that. To win it three times on the trot is a magnificent achievement – there aren't many teams who have managed that in the history of the game, and this season we've got the chance to do it four times in a row which would put us out on our own as the only side to have ever done that."

WERE YOU SURPRISED TO WIN THE PREMIERSHIP SO EASILY?
"I was, because I think if you look at the teams we expected to be up there with at the end – Chelsea, Leeds, Arsenal and Liverpool – they were all capable of putting a run together and challenging strongly, just as they will be next year."

WHY DO YOU THINK YOU WON THE LEAGUE BY SUCH A BIG MARGIN?
"Personally, I think experience is telling in this league and part of that is the ability to grind out results when you're not at your best. We struggled at times, but give or take the odd goal, even when we played poorly we managed to come away with three points from the game."

THE SEASON EFFECTIVELY ENDED FOR UNITED WHEN YOU WENT OUT OF EUROPE, DIDN'T IT?
"Yeah, it did. It happened the year before when we got beaten by Real Madrid – the season just fizzled out for us – so we wanted to make sure that didn't happen again. Going into the second leg against Bayern Munich we knew we had more or less won the league, so we knew that our season depended on the game, but Bayern beat us and that was that."

MATCHfacts RATINGS

PLAYED	STARS	AVERAGE
27	9	7.33

2

ROY KEANE
Manchester United

Age: 30 **Position:** Midfield

Lowdown: Keane continued his excellent form in Man. United's midfield in 2000-01. There were no treble wins or Player Of The Year awards this time around, but he was still the inspiration in the team as United coasted to their seventh league title in the last nine years. The captain finished the campaign with an average rating of 7.32 – just 0.01 behind team-mate Ryan Giggs – and his powerful performances earned him four star ratings in a team full of star names. Keane was always the driving force in the centre of the park, urging his team-mates to improve their efforts even when the league title seemed wrapped up by Christmas. Most notably, the skipper gave his colleagues a kick up the backside before the Champions League Quarter-Final against Bayern Munich. Going into the second leg after a 1-0 defeat at Old Trafford, the Irishman declared in MATCH that 'Heads would roll' at the club if United crashed out of the competition. The world's Press picked up on his comments, but he was even more scathing and vociferous when United did lose the tie, claiming they were an 'average' side. Keane knows Alex Ferguson's team needs added bite if they want to make the step-up from being a team of great players to a group of United legends, but he's just the man to take them there.

MATCH facts RATINGS

PLAYED	STARS	AVERAGE
28	4	7.32

3

JOE COLE
West Ham United

Age: 20 **Position:** Midfield

Lowdown: Cole can look back on 2000-01 as his breakthrough season. After bursting on the scene in the previous campaign, big things were expected of the midfielder and he started off in blistering fashion. An injury against Newcastle in October sidelined him for two months but his tricks helped West Ham reach the FA Cup Quarter-Finals and his 11 star ratings saw him claim two Matchman Of The Month awards. However, he struggled along with the team towards the end of the season, seeing his average drop to 7.25.

MATCH facts RATINGS

PLAYED	STARS	AVERAGE
27	11	7.25

4

PAOLO DI CANIO
West Ham United

Age: 33 **Position:** Striker

Lowdown: The Italian always earns high match ratings due to his importance to the West Ham team and the endless tricks he has up his sleeve. The 2000-01 season saw di Canio linked with a move to Lazio, but he pledged his future to the club by dying his hair claret. He played an important part in West Ham's surprising FA Cup Third Round victory at Man. United and won December's Matchman award. He comes fourth behind team mate Joe Cole, with the same average of 7.25 but appearing in four more games. The home fans wish he could have been an ever-present though after seven star ratings in 31 games.

MATCH facts RATINGS

PLAYED	STARS	AVERAGE
31	7	7.25

5

SOL CAMPBELL
Tottenham Hotspur

Age: 27 **Position:** Defence

Lowdown: Fitness problems ruled Campbell out for over half of the 2000-01 campaign and he suffered an injury in the FA Cup Semi-Final against rivals Arsenal which probably cost Spurs the game. Sol was sidelined for over a third of the season, but in his 21 league games he was at his dominating best – munching strikers for breakfast with the kind of ease that tempted a host of clubs to offer him lucrative contracts in the summer.

MATCH facts RATINGS

PLAYED	STARS	AVERAGE
21	6	7.23

6

SAMI HYYPIA
Liverpool

Age: 28 **Position:** Defence

Lowdown: Sami Hyypia was Liverpool's most consistent player last season. The giant Finn seems to improve with every year in the Premiership and his £3 million transfer in 1999 still looks a bargain. Impressively dominating in the air and comfortable on the ball, his partnership with Stephane Henchoz helped The Reds to their treble and earned Hyypia an average rating of 7.20.

MATCH facts RATINGS

PLAYED	STARS	AVERAGE
35	3	7.20

7

MARK VENUS
Ipswich Town

Age: 34 **Position:** Defence

Lowdown: Mark Venus might be coming towards the end of his career, but he's proved that he can produce the goods in the top-flight. The experienced defender scored the first goal in the Premiership last season – a superb free-kick at Tottenham – and didn't look back from that moment on. His consistency is reflected in his average rating of 7.20, which he achieved despite not being guaranteed a place in the first team by boss George Burley. Venus has agreed an extension to his contract which takes him to the end of 2002, to the delight of the Town faithful.

MATCH facts RATINGS

PLAYED	STARS	AVERAGE
24	3	7.20

8

JOHN McGREAL
Ipswich Town

Age: 29 **Position:** Defence

Lowdown: A second top ten ranking for an Ipswich player. The 2000-01 campaign was McGreal's first in the top flight, but he never looked overawed or out of his depth and he didn't struggle against more illustrious opponents in the Premiership. In fact, the former Tranmere Rovers defender seemed to thrive on the higher standard, a fact borne out by his two star ratings and his mighty 7.19 average. He even scored his first goal for the club against Everton – not bad going for a boyhood Liverpool fan!

MATCH facts RATINGS

PLAYED	STARS	AVERAGE
26	2	7.19

9

PATRICK VIEIRA
Arsenal

Age: 25 **Position:** Midfield

Lowdown: Vieira's contribution to Arsenal's 2000-01 campaign cannot be underestimated. His combination of skill, aggression and passion were first-class as he drove Arsenal into second place in the Premiership, the FA Cup Final and the quarter-finals of the Champions League. His temperament improved after two early red cards and he chipped in with some vital goals, notably a last-minute equaliser against Spurs. The midfield colossus earned nine star ratings from 30 Premiership games.

MATCH facts RATINGS

PLAYED	STARS	AVERAGE
30	9	7.16

10

STEVEN GERRARD
Liverpool

Age: 21 **Position:** Midfield

Lowdown: A defining season for the young midfielder. Despite concern over his niggling injuries Gerrard played in 33 Premiership games and earned seven star ratings for his all-action displays. He scored some memorable and vital goals, including a 30-yard screamer against Man. United. Named the PFA Young Player Of The Year, he also matured into an England regular in 2000-01, but he's a level-headed person who knows he has a lot to learn – citing Roy Keane and Patrick Vieira as two of his role models.

MATCH facts RATINGS		
PLAYED	SR	AVERAGE
33	7	7.15

11

PAUL MERSON
Aston Villa

Age: 33 **Position:** Midfield

Lowdown: In arguably the best form of his career, Merson had a fantastic 2000-01 season. The creative midfielder played in all of Villa's 38 Premiership games and was named the star man of the side an incredible 18 times. He finished second in October's Matchman Of The Month award.

MATCH facts RATINGS		
PLAYED	SR	AVERAGE
38	18	7.10

12

NOLBERTO SOLANO
Newcastle United

Age: 27 **Position:** Midfield

Lowdown: 'Nobby' continued to be as inspirational as he was frustrating for The Magpies in the 2000-01 season. Doubts about his loyalty sat alongside an impressive nine star ratings, but his dazzling wing play was always loved by the Toon Army.

MATCH facts RATINGS		
PLAYED	STARS	AVERAGE
32	9	7.09

14

15

DEAN KIELY
Charlton Athletic

Age: 30 **Position:** Goalkeeper

Lowdown: Kiely could have found himself even higher in the reckoning had a groin injury not ruled him out in January. Four star ratings and a 7.08 average proved the Charlton stopper could more than hold his own against the Premiership's best.

MATCH facts RATINGS		
PLAYED	STARS	AVERAGE
25	4	7.08

13

GARY WALSH
Bradford City

Age: 33 **Position:** Goalkeeper

Lowdown: Despite Bradford's leaky defence, Walsh enjoyed a solid season in goal – apart from a nightmare error against Man. United. With nine star ratings, he atoned for his error many times over but it wasn't enough to save The Bantams.

MATCH facts RATINGS		
PLAYED	STARS	AVERAGE
22	9	7.09

RICHARD RUFUS
Charlton Athletic

Age: 26 **Position:** Defence

Lowdown: The Addicks star had a great campaign, with 32 games under his belt and two goals against Coventry and Ipswich to help Charlton to tenth place in their first season back in the top flight. Unsung hero with four star ratings.

MATCH facts RATINGS		
PLAYED	STARS	AVERAGE
32	4	7.09

16

THOMAS SORENSEN
Sunderland

Age: 25 **Position:** Goalkeeper

Lowdown: Sorensen will go down in Sunderland folklore for one act – saving Alan Shearer's last-minute penalty to win the derby game against Newcastle at St James' Park. His overall form has been a major factor in The Black Cats' success.

MATCH facts RATINGS		
PLAYED	STARS	AVERAGE
34	3	7.08

17

CLAUS JENSEN
Charlton Athletic

Age: 24 **Position:** Midfield

Lowdown: The third Charlton player inside the top 20, Jensen enjoyed a wonderful first season after joining The Addicks from Bolton. An ever-present in the side, he provided ammunition for the two frontmen with some fantastic passing, notching six goals and nine star ratings!

MATCH facts RATINGS		
PLAYED	STARS	AVERAGE
38	9	7.07

18

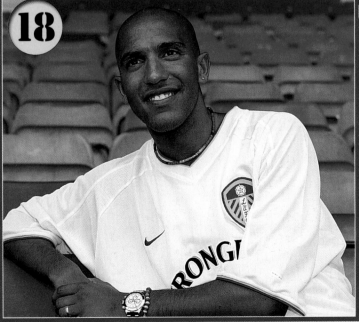

OLIVIER DACOURT
Leeds United

Age: 26 **Position:** Midfield

Lowdown: When he arrived at Elland Road last summer, Leeds fans still had the memory of Dacourt being sent-off for Everton against The Whites in 1998-99. But a scintillating 2000-01 campaign followed, instilling new memories in the minds of the Leeds faithful. His winning free-kick against Arsenal and his goal at Everton in February were just two of his many highlights. Dacourt is the highest-rated Leeds player in the MATCHfacts Top 50 with nine star ratings and deserves credit for his strong displays at home and in Europe after forming a formidable midfield partnership with David Batty. Widely praised for his 100 per cent commitment to the Leeds cause, he's certainly won over the Elland Road fans and they'll be desperate to keep him after overtures from abroad.

MATCH facts RATINGS		
PLAYED	STARS	AVERAGE
33	9	7.06

19

LEE BOWYER
Leeds United

Age: 24 **Position:** Midfield

Lowdown: Despite some well publicised problems away from football, Lee Bowyer had his best ever season for Leeds in 2000-01. Covering every blade of grass, he challenged for every ball possible and was the club's leading scorer in the Champions League, weighing in with some crucial goals – most notably at Elland Road against AC Milan. Leeds' ever-present Player Of The Season was rewarded with 12 star ratings and finished with a superb average rating of 7.05.

MATCH facts RATINGS

PLAYED	STARS	AVERAGE
38	12	7.05

20

SHAY GIVEN
Newcastle United

Age: 25 **Position:** Goalkeeper

Lowdown: Newcastle fans always feel that little bit more assured when they see Given's name on the teamsheet. He requested a transfer midway through the 2000-01 season but soon decided against the decision and was in sparkling form after that. Refreshingly for The Magpies, he also stayed injury-free and was kept on his toes by understudy Steve Harper, who impressed when he played. The Republic Of Ireland international was first-choice though and a colossus beween the sticks, as his stats prove.

MATCH facts RATINGS

PLAYED	STARS	AVERAGE
34	7	7.05

21

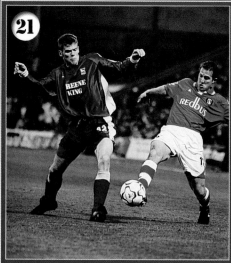

CRAIG BURLEY
Derby County

22

Age: 30 **Position:** Midfield

Lowdown: The performances of Scotland international Craig Burley provided Derby fans with some of the few highlights in an otherwise disappointing season. Despite missing the first six weeks of the new campaign through injury, the competitive Scot returned to add steel in the middle of the park and it was no coincidence that Derby's form lifted with his presence. Six star ratings illustrated his importance to the team and although he only scored two goals in the campaign, they included a vital winner against Sunderland.

MATCH facts RATINGS

PLAYED	STARS	AVERAGE
24	6	7.04

TIM FLOWERS
Leicester City

23

Age: 34 **Position:** Goalkeeper

Lowdown: Last season was a mixed one for the goalkeeper who has become a cult hero at Filbert Street. Six clean sheets in the first eight games helped take Leicester to the top of the Premiership table and Flowers's fantastic contribution continued over the festive period. But an unfortunate injury in the New Year's Day defeat at home to Bradford saw the ex-England stopper sidelined for over three months. He returned for the last three games of the season and reminded Foxes fans what they had missed in his absence.

MATCH facts RATINGS

PLAYED	STARS	AVERAGE
22	4	7.04

HERMANN HREIDARSSON
Ipswich Town

Age: 27 **Position:** Defence

Lowdown: Hreidarsson arrived at Portman Road as the club's record signing just two days before the start of 2000-01 and soon went about justifying his £4 million price tag. His surging runs and no-nonsense style were a big factor in the club's success last season and fans will be pleased to know that his contract runs until 2005. The defender is a real favourite at Portman Road and his hero status was cemented by his bizarre goal celebrations against Bradford, when he dived head long into the North Stand.

MATCH facts RATINGS

PLAYED	STARS	AVERAGE
35	3	7.05

24

DEAN RICHARDS
Southampton

Age: 27 **Position:** Defence

Lowdown: Richards proved to be one of the most effective centre-backs in the Premiership over the 2000-01 season. He was strong in the air, tough in the tackle and scored his fair share of important goals from set-pieces. Glenn Hoddle had a particularly positive effect on the former England Under-21 international and his dominance in defence was a big factor in The Saints' consistent form.

MATCH facts RATINGS

PLAYED	STARS	AVERAGE
28	8	7.03

25

JAMIE CLAPHAM
Ipswich Town

Age: 26 **Position:** Midfield

Lowdown: The first half of the season saw Clapham emerge as a key player in Town's rise to the top six of the Premiership. His skill on the ball and tireless running secured him the left-wing birth as he was touted as a possible England candidate. By his own admission, his high standards began to drop at the end of the season, when he was often left on the bench because of Martijn Reuser's form. But that doesn't detract from four star ratings and an average of 7.03. He'll want to get back to his best this season.

MATCH facts RATINGS

PLAYED	STARS	AVERAGE
31	4	7.03

26
TONY ADAMS
Arsenal

Age: 35 **Position:** Defence

Lowdown: After announcing his retirement from international football, the Arsenal captain was able to focus his attention on domestic matters. He was once again an inspiration at the heart of The Gunners' defence and the team certainly suffered when he was out injured.

| MATCH facts | | RATINGS |
PLAYED	STARS	AVERAGE
26	0	7.03

27
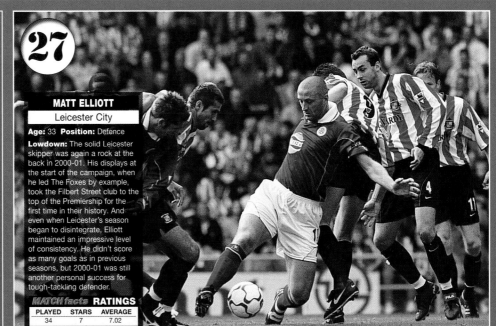

MATT ELLIOTT
Leicester City

Age: 33 **Position:** Defence

Lowdown: The solid Leicester skipper was again a rock at the back in 2000-01. His displays at the start of the campaign, when he led The Foxes by example, took the Filbert Street club to the top of the Premiership for the first time in their history. And even when Leicester's season began to disintegrate, Elliott maintained an impressive level of consistency. He didn't score as many goals as in previous seasons, but 2000-01 was still another personal success for tough-tackling defender.

| MATCH facts | | RATINGS |
PLAYED	STARS	AVERAGE
34	7	7.02

28

NEIL SULLIVAN
Tottenham Hotspur

Age: 31 **Position:** Goalkeeper

Lowdown: Having joined Spurs in the summer on a Bosman free transfer, Sullivan was seen as a replacement for Ian Walker. But he still had to perform to be certain of his place and that's what the Scotland international did all season. A tremendous shot-stopper who proved to be comfortable and reliable in the air, he had excellent games in the matches against Arsenal and West Ham in the FA Cup. He made vital saves to earn an improbable win at Upton Park and defied The Gunners almost single-handedly in the semi-final to prevent what could have been an embarrassing scoreline. While Spurs fans should thank him for that, England supporters should lament the fact that he chose to represent Scotland rather than England, the country of his birth. Deserved all of his seven star ratings last season.

| MATCH facts | | RATINGS |
PLAYED	STARS	AVERAGE
35	7	7.00

29

RIO FERDINAND
Leeds United

Age: 22 **Position:** Defence

Lowdown: Leeds' £18 million man fully justified his transfer fee with some stirling displays at centre-back. With six star ratings, Ferdinand continued to improve last term, scoring against former club West Ham and impressing with England.

| MATCH facts | | RATINGS |
PLAYED	STARS	AVERAGE
35	6	7.00

30

HORACIO CARBONARI
Derby County

Age: 28 **Position:** Defence

Lowdown: Despite receiving two red cards in September, the Argentinian defender deserves his top 50 place after being one of Derby's best players as they avoided the drop, notching up an impressive 7.00 average in a difficult season for The Rams.

| MATCH facts | | RATINGS |
PLAYED	STARS	AVERAGE
27	5	7.00

31
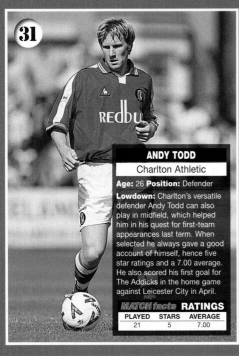

ANDY TODD
Charlton Athletic

Age: 26 **Position:** Defender

Lowdown: Charlton's versatile defender Andy Todd can also play in midfield, which helped him in his quest for first-team appearances last term. When selected he always gave a good account of himself, hence five star ratings and a 7.00 average. He also scored his first goal for The Addicks in the home game against Leicester City in April.

| MATCH facts | | RATINGS |
PLAYED	STARS	AVERAGE
21	5	7.00

32

JAMES SCOWCROFT
Ipswich Town

Age: 29 **Position:** Midfield

Lowdown: Ipswich Town's 1999-2000 Player Of The Year again proved how important he was to the team in the 2000-01 season, both in his preferred midfield position and as an out-and-out striker. The advanced role turned out to be another great tactical decision by boss George Burley, who seems to match all his squad's talents together perfectly. Scowcroft's aerial prowess made him an ideal partner for the smaller Marcus Stewart and he also improved on the ball. And when Alun Armstrong was signed in December he was able to move back to the right of midfield. He missed several games towards the end of the campaign with a groin injury, but still signed a new contract which will keep him playing at the club until 2004. He remains a key player at Portman Road.

| MATCH facts | | RATINGS |
PLAYED	STARS	AVERAGE
30	2	7.00

33

STEPHEN CARR
Tottenham Hotspur

Age: 25 **Position:** Defence

Lowdown: Tottenham's well-respected right-back suffered a seven-week spell out of action with a groin injury that led to an operation on a hernia. But he still appeared in 28 Premiership games for Spurs and was the star man on four occasions. His style of play, which sees him bursting forward in attacking positions, really caught the eye and led to interest from abroad. The Republic Of Ireland full-back also scored three league goals.

MATCH facts RATINGS

PLAYED	STARS	AVERAGE
28	4	6.96

34

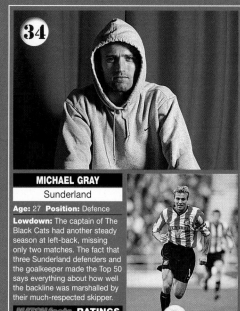

MICHAEL GRAY
Sunderland

Age: 27 **Position:** Defence

Lowdown: The captain of The Black Cats had another steady season at left-back, missing only two matches. The fact that three Sunderland defenders and the goalkeeper made the Top 50 says everything about how well the backline was marshalled by their much-respected skipper.

MATCH facts RATINGS

PLAYED	STARS	AVERAGE
36	4	6.94

35

MARTIJN REUSER
Ipswich Town

Age: 26 **Position:** Midfield

Lowdown: Ipswich midfielder Reuser got his chance to shine in the second half of the term and his energetic displays kept the previously impressive Jamie Clapham on the sidelines. The Dutchman was a real star as Town bagged a UEFA Cup spot.

MATCH facts RATINGS

PLAYED	STARS	AVERAGE
19	3	6.94

36

MART POOM
Derby County

Age: 29 **Position:** Goalkeeper

Lowdown: Derby's much-loved Estonia international once again impressed in the Premiership, earning seven star ratings for his outstanding all-round ability. Apart from his absence through injury in February and March, Poom remained the first-choice 'keeper at Pride Park and it's still a mystery why the big guns haven't tried to prise him away. Well regarded by all at Derby, Poom's displays between the sticks have been vital in helping the club to preserve its Premier League status since his bargain £500,000 transfer in 1997.

MATCH facts RATINGS

PLAYED	STARS	AVERAGE
33	7	6.93

37

JIM MAGILTON
Ipswich Town

Age: 32 **Position:** Midfield

Lowdown: As Ipswich's most experienced midfielder, Magilton provided a calming presence on the pitch in the 2000-01 season. The Irishman made up for his lack of pace with his intelligent passing and his ability to bring the ball out of defence to get the team moving forward. His fiery temper got the better of him occasionally – he received a one-match ban for comments made to the referee during the 4-1 defeat at Chelsea – but five star ratings are a big indication of his worth. Surely one of the surprises of the Premiership.

MATCH facts RATINGS

PLAYED	STARS	AVERAGE
33	5	6.93

38

MICHAEL BALL
Everton

Age: 22 **Position:** Defence

Lowdown: Ball had another solid season in a struggling team at Goodison Park. Walter Smith tried him at centre-back because of an injury-crisis and he never looked back, filling the role as if he'd played there for years. Calm and collected on the ball, he was regularly linked with a move away from Everton but this didn't affect his form. He even earned his first senior England call-up for the friendly tie against Spain at Villa Park. He acquitted himself well for the Three Lions and will be looking for more caps in the future.

MATCH facts RATINGS

PLAYED	STARS	AVERAGE
29	2	6.93

39

KIERON DYER
Newcastle United

Age: 23 **Position:** Midfield

Lowdown: Despite suffering with shin splints for a large part of 2000-01, this was the season that confirmed Dyer as one of the hottest properties in English football. He demonstrated pace, skill and vision in abundance, leading to interest from all the top clubs. But Bobby Robson wasn't swayed and it's easy to see why. Dyer was delightful to watch, effortlessly floating past defenders to set up and score some truly memorable goals. There is surely more to come from Dyer, but he undoubtedly doubled his value in 2000-01.

MATCH facts RATINGS

PLAYED	STARS	AVERAGE
26	4	6.92

40

TITUS BRAMBLE
Ipswich Town

Age: 20 **Position:** Defence

Lowdown: Since the age of 15, Bramble had been hampered by injuries, but the 2000-01 season allowed him to break free from his problems and deliver on the field. His composure on the ball belied his age and experience, and he is already being touted as the next big-money name to come out of the Ipswich youth system. He was only chosen as the star man three times, but in a team bristling with talent that was no mean achievement. This player is definitely one to watch!

MATCH facts RATINGS

PLAYED	STARS	AVERAGE
26	3	6.92

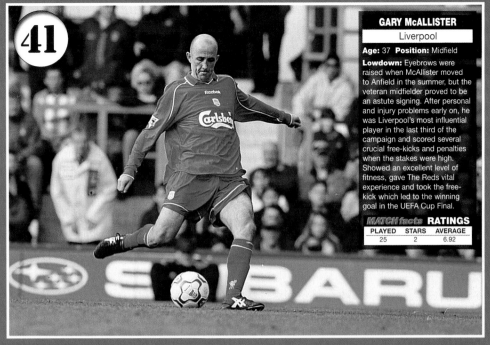

41

GARY McALLISTER
Liverpool

Age: 37 **Position:** Midfield

Lowdown: Eyebrows were raised when McAllister moved to Anfield in the summer, but the veteran midfielder proved to be an astute signing. After personal and injury problems early on, he was Liverpool's most influential player in the last third of the campaign and scored several crucial free-kicks and penalties when the stakes were high. Showed an excellent level of fitness, gave The Reds vital experience and took the free-kick which led to the winning goal in the UEFA Cup Final.

MATCHfacts RATINGS

PLAYED	STARS	AVERAGE
25	2	6.92

42

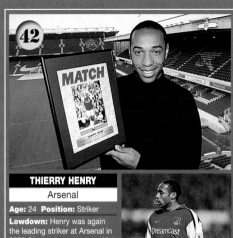

THIERRY HENRY
Arsenal

Age: 24 **Position:** Striker

Lowdown: Henry was again the leading striker at Arsenal in 2000-01, scoring some cracking goals – most notably a superb strike against Man. United at Highbury. His pace and flair made him a constant threat in attack, leading to 17 league goals and five star ratings.

MATCHfacts RATINGS

PLAYED	STARS	AVERAGE
32	5	6.87

43

DAVID BECKHAM
Manchester United

Age: 26 **Position:** Midfield

Lowdown: It was another satisfying season for Becks, who helped United to capture another Premiership title and took on the England captaincy. He featured in 31 league games, with four star ratings, and was regularly in contention for the Matchman Of The Month award.

MATCHfacts RATINGS

PLAYED	STARS	AVERAGE
31	4	6.87

44

PAUL INCE
Middlesbrough

Age: 34 **Position:** Midfield

Lowdown: When the going gets tough, the tough get going and that certainly applied to Paul Ince last season. As Boro stared Division One in the face their hard-man skipper led by example and was in fantastic form as they escaped the drop.

MATCHfacts RATINGS

PLAYED	STARS	AVERAGE
30	6	6.86

45

PAUL SCHOLES
Manchester United

Age: 26 **Position:** Midfield

Lowdown: United's midfield diamond had another influential season, earning four star ratings from 29 matches. His runs from deep brought six league goals, and six more in 12 Champions League games demonstrated his appetite for the big games.

MATCHfacts RATINGS

PLAYED	STARS	AVERAGE
29	4	6.86

46

MATT HOLLAND
Ipswich Town

Age: 27 **Position:** Midfield

Lowdown: The club captain went from strength to strength last season – his remarkable record of starting in more than 200 consecutive games for Ipswich gave him an incredible average of 6.86. A vital cog in Town's well-oiled machine.

MATCHfacts RATINGS

PLAYED	STARS	AVERAGE
38	2	6.86

47

JULIO ARCA
Sunderland

Age: 20 **Position:** Midfield

Lowdown: Arca proved to be an exciting member of Peter Reid's impressive Sunderland team last season. The talented young midfielder played with plenty of intelligence and guts to become a real favourite with the Black Cats faithful.

MATCHfacts RATINGS

PLAYED	STARS	AVERAGE
27	4	6.85

48

JODY CRADDOCK
Sunderland

Age: 26 **Position:** Defence

Lowdown: Virtually unknown in the Premiership before the start of the campaign, Craddock was a suprise plus for Sunderland at the heart of their defence. His control of the powerful Jimmy Floyd Hasselbaink in a 4-2 win at Chelsea was a big highlight.

MATCHfacts RATINGS

PLAYED	STARS	AVERAGE
34	5	6.85

50

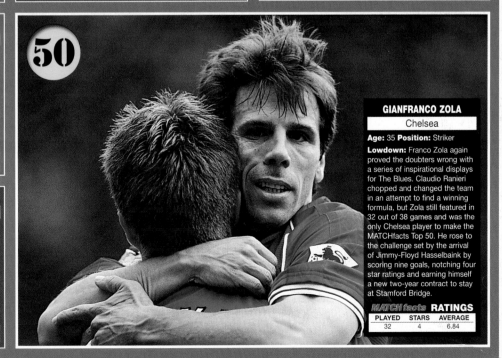

GIANFRANCO ZOLA
Chelsea

Age: 35 **Position:** Striker

Lowdown: Franco Zola again proved the doubters wrong with a series of inspirational displays for The Blues. Claudio Ranieri chopped and changed the team in an attempt to find a winning formula, but Zola still featured in 32 out of 38 games and was the only Chelsea player to make the MATCHfacts Top 50. He rose to the challenge set by the arrival of Jimmy-Floyd Hasselbaink by scoring nine goals, notching four star ratings and earning himself a new two-year contract to stay at Stamford Bridge.

MATCHfacts RATINGS

PLAYED	STARS	AVERAGE
32	4	6.84

49

ROBBIE SAVAGE
Leicester City

Age: 27 **Position:** Midfield

Lowdown: Savage seemed to come of age last season under Peter Taylor's leadership. The Wales midfielder showed more to his game than his all-action reputation and he took on more creative responsibility after Neil Lennon's departure to Celtic.

MATCHfacts RATINGS

PLAYED	STARS	AVERAGE
33	6	6.84

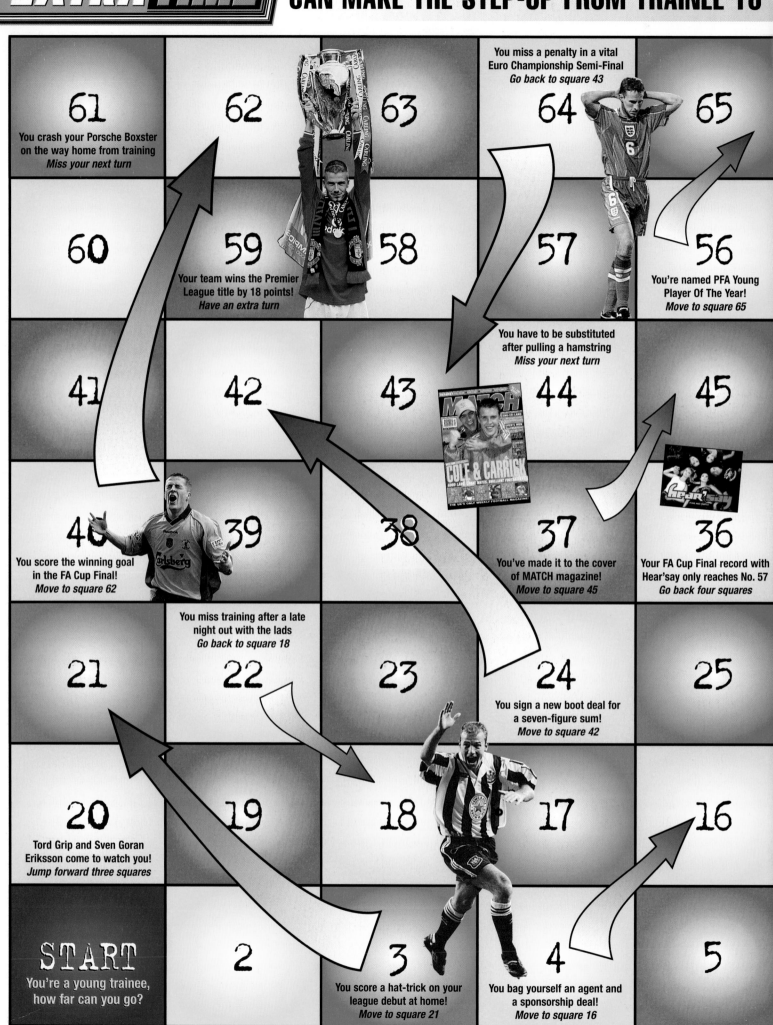

61
You crash your Porsche Boxster on the way home from training
Miss your next turn

62

63

64
You miss a penalty in a vital Euro Championship Semi-Final
Go back to square 43

65

60

59
Your team wins the Premier League title by 18 points!
Have an extra turn

58

57

56
You're named PFA Young Player Of The Year!
Move to square 65

41

42

43

44
You have to be substituted after pulling a hamstring
Miss your next turn

45

40
You score the winning goal in the FA Cup Final!
Move to square 62

39

38

37
You've made it to the cover of MATCH magazine!
Move to square 45

36
Your FA Cup Final record with Hear'say only reaches No. 57
Go back four squares

21

22
You miss training after a late night out with the lads
Go back to square 18

23

24
You sign a new boot deal for a seven-figure sum!
Move to square 42

25

20
Tord Grip and Sven Goran Eriksson come to watch you!
Jump forward three squares

19

18

17

16

START
You're a young trainee, how far can you go?

2

3
You score a hat-trick on your league debut at home!
Move to square 21

4
You bag yourself an agent and a sponsorship deal!
Move to square 16

5

66

67 You try to bag a pop star wife, but end up with Jordan
Go back to square 35

68

69

FINISH You're a football legend!

55

54

53

52

51 You're fined a week's wages for having a 'Beckham' mohican
Go back to square 49

46

47

48

49

50 You're dropped in favour of Hamilton Ricard
Go back to square 30

35

34 You impress on your full England debut!
Move to square 53

33 You're sent-off for pushing the referee to the floor
Go back to square 6

32

31

26 You score on your debut for England's Under-21s!
Jump forward four squares

27

28

29 Belly's gonna get ya! Your gaffer sees you in a kebab shop
Miss your next turn

30

15

14 You're recognised in the local supermarket!
Have an extra turn

13

12

11 You move to Everton and suffer a nightmare injury
Go back to square one

6

7

8

9 You've sealed a move to a Premiership club!
Move to square 28

10

ENGLAND

THE FINAL WHISTLE ANSWERS

Here's where we identify the real footy fans from the wannabes, where we separate the budding stattos from the mere armchair fans! The moment of truth is upon us, as you check off your scores to find out what kind of trophy you're worthy of. So do you deserve a World Cup winners' medal or a free transfer?

261-300
YOU'VE WON THE WORLD CUP!

What a star! You certainly know your football and all your mates have now nicknamed you 'Statto'. Not only do you go actually go to watch matches, you also have that very rare textbook knowledge of the beautiful game!

221-260
YOU'VE WON THE CHAMPIONS LEAGUE!

Very good! You may not have your head stuck in statistics books, but you can talk a good game. You know who did what, where, when and by how much… but you didn't go all the way and buy the T-shirt!

176-220
YOU'VE WON THE FA CUP!

Not bad! Okay, maybe there were a few hard questions in there, so we'll let you off because that was a good showing. To improve though, you'll need to get better at remembering all those faces, dates and places!

131-175
YOU'VE WON THE LEAGUE CUP!

A respectable result! Your knowledge of your own football club is good, but you don't know very much about other teams. That's not a bad thing, but it won't win you any quiz prizes!

86-130
YOU'VE WON THE SECOND DIVISION!

We're not impressed! You haven't even managed to get half the points available! But don't cry yet, because you've shown enough potential to give us some hope. Just make sure you learn from all of your mistakes!

41-85
YOU'VE WON THE LDV VANS TROPHY!

You're not singing any more! What kind of dodgy performance was that? If you're under eight years old, that may be acceptable – but if you're not, you need serious coaching! You can start by doing all the questions again!

under 40
YOU'VE WON A FREE TRANSFER!

Hello? Do you actually like football? If so, sorry – but what an absolutely shocking performance. There's just no excuse for this kind of score. Order yourself a subscription to MATCH and start learning quickly!

Final Whistle One — page 28

FIRST XI

1
2
3
4
5
6
7
8
9
10
11

CODE BREAKER

1

Alan Shearer.

SAY WHAT?

1

Robbie Fowler.

CIVVY STREET

1

Jon Harley.

WHO PLAYS WHERE?

1
2
3
4
5
6
7
8
9

1. C; 2. D; 3. A; 4. E; 5. B; 6. F; 7. F; 8. G; 9. H.

WHO AM I?

1

Michael Carrick.

Final Whistle Two — page 48

SECOND XI

1
2
3
4
5
6
7
8
9
10
11

CROSSWORD

1   Out of 34 points I scored...

REF OFF

1

Pierluigi Collina.

WHO WON IT?

1

Everton.

WHOSE NUMBER?

1
2
3
4
5

1. Eleven; 2. Nine; 3. Fourteen; 4. Ten; 5. Five.

THE GAFFERS

1.
2.
3.
4.
5.

1. Dave Jones; 2. Four (FA Cup, League Cup, European Cup-Winners' Cup & European Super Cup); 3. Liverpool; 4. True; 5. Bournemouth, Southampton & Blackburn.

CONNECTIONS

1.

Sheffield Wednesday.

CODE BREAKER

1.

Dennis Wise.

Final Whistle Three — page 60

THIRD XI

1.
2.
3.
4.
5.
6.
7.
8.
9.
10.
11.

1. AS Roma; 2. 1989-90; 3. Sunderland; 4. Five; 5. Mexico; 6. Robbie Fowler & Stan Collymore; 7. 335 goals & Leeds; 8. True; 9. Roy Evans; 10. £11 million; 11. Bradford City.

FORMER CLUBS

1.
2.
3.
4.
5.

1. Nottingham Forest; 2. Wimbledon; 3. QPR; 4. Inter Milan; 5. Watford.

WHO'S MISSING?

1.
2.

Martin Keown, Paul Ince.

GUESS THE PLAYERS

1.
2.
3.

Tim Flowers, Francis Jeffers & Steven Gerrard.

DATING AGENCY

1.

Nicky Weaver.

CODE BREAKER

1.

Paolo di Canio.

Final Whistle Four — page 80

FOURTH XI

1.
2.
3.
4.
5.
6.
7.
8.
9.
10.
11.

1. Moscow Dynamo; 2. True; 3. Mark Hateley; 4. Leeds; 5. Ally McCoist; 6. Newcastle, Tottenham & Lazio; 7. 1997; 8. Walter Smith, PSV Eindhoven; 9. St. Johnstone & Celtic; 10. 17 goals, including three penalties; 11. £12 million from Chelsea.

CROSSWORD

1. Out of 34 points I scored...

ACROSS: 8. Goma; 9. Thome; 10. Alex; 11. Lomas; 12. O'Neill; 13. Carragher; 15. Brown; 18. Jeffers; 20. Gardner; 23. James; 25. Gillespie; 28. Ehiogu; 30. Agent; 32. Bell; 33. Prior; 34. Okon.
DOWN: 1. Port Vale; 2. Taylor; 3. Stam; 4. Roussel; 5. Defoe; 6. Lane; 7. Yellow; 14. Gers; 16. Red; 17. Bali; 19. Foe; 21. Eriksson; 22. Di Canio; 24. Ashley; 26. Sutton; 27. Guppy; 29. Owls; 31. Eire.

SAY WHAT?

1.

Dennis Bergkamp.

REF OFF

1.

Paul Durkin.

WHO WON IT?

1.

A. Arsenal.

CONNECTIONS

1.

Both were managed by Alex Ferguson.

NAME THE CLUB

1.

Bradford City.

CIVVY STREET

1.

Robbie Savage.

Final Whistle Five — page 92

FIFTH XI

1.
2.
3.
4.
5.
6.
7.
8.
9.
10.
11.

1. 1972 & Arsenal; 2. Don Revie; 3. Brian Clough; 4. Gordon Strachan; 5. Nimes & Man. United; 6. Aston Villa & 3-0; 7. True – 26 goals in 38 games in 1996-97; 8. 34 league goals; 9. Eirik Bakke & Olivier Dacourt; 10. Tottenham; 11. Alan Smith.

CODE BREAKER

1.

David Beckham.

1-0

1.
2.
3.
4.
5.

1. Roberto di Matteo; 2. Alan Shearer; 3. Thierry Henry; 4. Dietmar Hamann; 5. Paolo di Canio.

WHO WON IT?

1.

Real Madrid.

ALL NATIONS

1.
2.
3.
4.
5.

1. Czech Republic; 2. Portugal; 3. Slovenia; 4. Spain; 5. Denmark.

WHO AM I?

1.

David Seaman.

MEGA WORDSPOT – FINAL WHISTLE 1

Out of 35 points I scored...

MEGA WORDSPOT – FINAL WHISTLE 3

Out of 35 points I scored...

MEGA WORDSPOT – FINAL WHISTLE 5

Out of 35 points I scored...

Graeme Le Saux lines up with the three contestants in the Fan Of The Year final.

Ray Parlour meets the International Final competitors.

The 'Football Fever' crew with Nicola, James & Jo.

Our Graeme sits in Gary Lineker's 'MOTD' seat to pose the final questions.

FAN OF THE YEAR 2001!

Check out how the best young fans in Britain fared in the **MATCH** & **Nationwide** Fan Of The Year finals!

HUNDREDS OF FANS ACROSS THE COUNTRY scribbled frantically to prepare their entry forms when applications opened for the MATCH and Nationwide Building Society Fan Of The Year 2000-01 competition. In only its second year, the only national competition for young fans attracted vast interest and the judging panel – which included star names Martin Keown and Mark Bright – whittled the entries down to just six people.

Three shortlisted fans in the International Fan category took part in a tense final in the MATCH offices with an international season ticket up for grabs – that's a pair of tickets to every home England or Scotland game for a period of two years! Arsenal and England midfielder Ray Parlour came along to play quizmaster, asking the three fans – James O'Donnell, Nicola Hill and Victoria Thornton – hard questions to test their footy knowledge.

After answering 12 questions each, Victoria finally bowed out – leaving James and Nicola to fight it out. Then, in a tough tie-breaker, Nicola's excellent knowledge shone through to win! **"It was very nerve-wracking for the kids and you could see that in their faces, but it was very enjoyable,"** said Parlour. **"I think the competition's a very good idea. There are a lot of dedicated fans out there who follow their clubs, but they don't get any recognition, so it's nice to do this. It's a great opportunity for the fans and I'm sure the winner's really nervous about being in the overall final now!"**

Meeting Nicola in the final was the Club Fan Of The Year – the winner of which was decided through another tough football knowledge quiz. The three fans who made it through to the Club Fan Final had each shown an incredible level of dedication – working hard in their spare time to pay for match tickets and going to games in the face of adversity. In the contest, Plymouth fan Jo Benwell scored top marks to beat both Karla Wrigly, who supports Oldham and Wolves fan Paul Mansell, to the prize of a club season ticket. Scotland fan James O'Donnell also qualified as runner-up.

The overall grand final was filmed in the 'Match Of The Day' studios and was shown on BBC1's 'Football Fever' show. This time Chelsea left-back Graeme Le Saux took over the reigns as quizmaster and he was surprised by the standard of the contestants. **"Youngsters are always into their sport and I thought their knowledge was excellent,"** he said.

Jo's knowledge of Plymouth shone through with a 12/12 mark, beating Nicola into second and James into third. She won a Fan Of The Year trophy to take back to Plymouth, but wanted to pass her luck on to the team. **"I just hope Argyle can match my success next season,"** she said. **I expect them to be the Team Of The Year in 2002!"**

Watch out for details of how you can enter the 2001-02 competition in a forthcoming issue of MATCH.

MATCH readers and West Ham fanatics **HANNAH MARSHALL** and **CHRISTINE LESTER** are seen pictured with goalkeeper **STEPHEN BYWATER**.

TOM DRAKE from Yorkshire is obsessed with Liverpool – as you can see from his bedroom! His memorabilia collection includes Owen's autograph.

NICK HOWSON is photographed with former footy stars **MARK BRIGHT** and **IAN WRIGHT**, having met them at the Radio Five Live studios.

MY BIG DAY OUT!

MATCH reader Holand Couzens enjoys a day out at Man. United's training ground!

HOLAND AND DANIEL ADMIRE THE FINE PIECES OF SILVERWARE AT MAN. UNITED!

THE NEXT GENERATION'S BECKS AND GIGGS? THE BOYS CAN ONLY DREAM...

HOLAND PRETENDS HE'S A SUPERSTAR AS HE'S INTERVIEWED FOR LOCAL TELEVISION!

DESTINATION: Manchester United's training ground, Carrington, Manchester

EVENT: Training & Tour

Warning: If you're a Manchester United fan, you may not want to read the following article because you may become extremely jealous! That's because reader Holand Couzens won the chance of a lifetime to watch his Manchester United heroes in training. He was also invited to sample life as a top young footballer at the club's famous youth academy – not bad, eh?

Eight-year-old Holand, from Lincolnshire, won the chance to visit United's Carrington training ground as part of a two-day trip to Manchester. He also got the chance to take a guided tour around Old Trafford and have dinner in the Red Café overlooking the pitch!

It was Holand's parents who entered the MATCH competition so he was amazed when he was told that he'd won! As the competition was run by McVitie's Jaffa Cakes – the sponsors of the United youth academy – Holand and his cousin Daniel were given some top training by the youth coaches and had the chance to play against other winners from across the country.

The winners all trained at United's old training ground, The Cliff, while Daniel's dad stayed overnight in a local hotel before going to watch Becks, Giggs, Keane and co. train the following day. It was a tough training session for The Red Devils because they had a hard Premiership game at home the next day, but Holand and Daniel watched them intensely to pick up some tips from the stars.

The boys were also given some Jaffa Cakes to take home, but they didn't last long – they scoffed the lot after a hard day's training!

IT WASN'T ALL FUN THOUGH, HOLAND HAD TO CLEAN BOOTS WHILE HE WAS THERE!

THE LADS GOT TO CHECK OUT THE GYM IN WHICH ROY KEANE PUMPS IRON!

ALL THE COMPETITION WINNERS HAD A GREAT TIME TRAINING AT UNITED!

PAUL ROWE, DANIEL DORLING, JOSHUA GOODALL & SCOTT LARGE had their picture taken while watching the England team training.

Middlesbrough supporter CECILY FEARNLEY is seen with one of her favourite players PAUL INCE. Cecily's an avid fan and enjoys playing footy too!

MATCH reader JAMES PUGH from Shrewsbury is a Blackburn fan as you can see from his wallpaper! Despite a long journey, he sees ten games a year.

STRANGE BUT FALSE!
David Beckham got the idea for his infamous Mohican haircut from his son Brooklyn, who sported the haircut at Old Trafford months before Becks had it done!

the JOKES on You!

Check out this bunch of footy jokes sent in by **MATCH** readers!

MANCHESTER CITY
Paulo Wanchope is out shopping and sees something interesting in the kitchen store. "What's that?" he asks. "A Thermos flask," replies the assistant. "What does it do?" The assistant tells him it keeps hot things hot and cold things cold. Really impressed, Wanchope buys one and takes it along to his next training session. The lads are impressed. "What does it do?" they ask. "It keeps hot things hot and cold things cold," says Wanchope. "And what have you got in it?" asks Nicky Weaver. And Wanchope replies: "Two cups of tea and a cornetto."
★ Sent in by Jonathan Wilkes, Exeter

NEWCASTLE UNITED
Q: Why does Alan Shearer drink his coffee out of a glass?
A: Because he's lost all the cups!
★ Sent in by Abi Farrell, e-mail

GENERAL FOOTBALL
Q: What does a footballer and a magician have in common?
A: They both do hat-tricks!
★ Sent in by David Howe, Brighton

PORTSMOUTH
Worried by all the expensive trips to Cardiff's Millennium Stadium come the end of the season? Frustrated by the length of the waiting lists for season tickets and fighting through the crowds to get out of the stadium come five o'clock on matchdays? Overcome the problem simply by supporting Portsmouth.
★ Sent in by Kevin Searle, Havant

MANCHESTER UNITED
A man is sent to hell as punishment for his sins. The devil meets him at the gate and escorts him to his place of torment. Along the way he passes a room where a Manchester United fan is having a deep conversation with a beautiful lady. "That's just not fair," said the man. "I have to live a life of pain and torture and that plonker gets to spend forever with that beautiful lady." The devil prods him with his fork and says: "Who are you to question that woman's punishment?"
★ Sent in by Dave, Purfleet

SEND YOUR JOKES OR PUNS TO: The Jokes On You, MATCH Magazine, Bushfield House, Orton Centre, Peterborough PE2 5UW.

FOOTY DAYS OUT!

MATCH looks at the best way to spend your weekends & holidays – enjoying football!

Museum Of Scottish Football

WHAT IS IT? It's a museum devoted to the history of the Scottish game. As well as hearing stories of games and days gone by, there's a replica press box and changing rooms to give a clearer picture.

WHERE IS IT? In the South Stand at Hampden Park in Glasgow, Scotland. If you have plenty of time, it only costs a few quid extra to do the stadium tour and check out the changing rooms!

PRICES: Entry to the museum is £5 for adults and £2.50 for children. The tour costs £2.50/£1.25 on top of that price.

OPENING HOURS: The museum is open Monday to Saturday from 10am-5pm and from 11am-5pm on Sundays. The tours around the stadium take place daily at: 11am, 12noon, 1pm, 2pm and 3pm. The museum is closed on matchdays though!

ANY GOOD? There's plenty of things to keep football fans of all ages occupied. There are several films and touch-screen features, while older fans can marvel at Kenny Dalglish's 100th international!

CONTACT: You can pay on the door, but it's best to book in advance if you want to go on the tour. Call (0141) 616 6100 for details or check out their website at: www.scottishfootballmuseum.org.uk

Millennium Stadium Tour

WHAT IS IT? How would you like to take a fascinating look behind the scenes at the national stadium of Wales? It's where Liverpool lifted the 2001 League Cup and FA Cup. The tour lets you find out more about the retractable roof and see the hundreds of names laid in paved stone on the Stadium Riverwalk.

WHERE IS IT? The stadium is in the centre of Cardiff, near to shops and local amenities. It is a short walk from the rail station and close to the M4 motorway.

PRICES: The tour costs £5 for adults, £2.50 for children and £3 for OAPs. Groups of 20 get a discount and a family ticket (two adults, three children) is £15.

OPENING HOURS: Starting at 10am from Mon-Sat, tours run regularly stopping at 5pm. On Sundays and Bank Holidays, the last tour is at 4.30pm. The tour does not run on Easter Sunday, Christmas Day, New Year's Day and on matchdays.

ANY GOOD? If you're a footy fanatic, you'll love this tour. You get a chance to see the stadium from a player's view, going into the changing rooms, medical room and walking down the tunnel!

CONTACT: Bookings must be made in advance, so call (029) 2082 2228.

Anfield Museum

WHAT IS IT? It's a museum devoted to Liverpool FC which takes a look back at the club's colourful history while celebrating recent players and their successes. There's a film called 'This is Anfield' which shows you what goes on at the club on a day-to-day basis and lots of interactive entertainment for children, including a penalty shoot-out machine.

WHERE IS IT? The museum is based at Anfield, near the front of the ground.

PRICES: An adult ticket costs £5. OAPs and children are charged £3. Members of the International Supporters Club and season ticket holders are given £1 off.

OPENING HOURS: The museum is open daily during office hours, but shuts one hour prior to kick-off on matchdays.

ANY GOOD? There's memorabilia to view from old kits, tickets and replica trophies – there have been a few of those lately! This is a must if you're a Liverpool fan and the museum is open on matchday, so it's worth arriving early to take a look.

CONTACT: You don't have to book in advance, but it's advisable to call them on (0151) 260 6677 as the museum is always busy. The staff on the tour can also cater for those with special needs.

National Football Museum

WHAT IS IT? After years of building and preparation work, the museum is finally open. You can find out how the game was invented, explore the time capsule of football's past and also have a game of table football, with action replays!

WHERE IS IT? The museum is based at Preston North End's Deepdale stadium.

PRICES: Entry costs £6.95 for adults and £4.95 for children aged 5-15 years old. Family tickets start at £19.95, rising to £24.95 for two adults and four children. Discounts for big groups are available on request, as are deals for schools.

OPENING HOURS: The museum is open Tuesday to Saturday from 10am-5pm and from 11am-5pm on Sundays. It remains open late – until 7.30pm – on midweek matchdays. But the museum is closed every Monday, except on Bank Holidays.

ANY GOOD? The museum has been given rave reviews in the national Press. It's split into sections – the First Half (history), Second Half (games and art gallery) and Final Whistle (shop and café).

CONTACT: You can pay upon entry or book on the 24-hour information line, which is (01772) 908 442. The museum is also accessible for wheelchair users.

We hope you've enjoyed the latest action-packed and fun-filled
MATCH annual. Now that you've tested yourself on the quizzes, seen what goes on behind the scenes in Premiership dressing rooms and read about the illustrious careers of four captains, it's time to look forward. 2002 promises to be a very exciting year – particularly with the World Cup Finals taking place in South Korea and Japan in the summer, by which time we'll know who won the race for the Premiership title! Remember, you can keep up-to-date with all the latest news and views in your weekly copy of MATCH magazine. We'll review all of footy's ups and downs in next year's Christmas annual, but if you've got any ideas for the 2003 annual, you can contact us at this address: MATCH, Bushfield House, Orton Centre, Peterborough, PE2 5UW.